Creating Drama with 4–7 Year Olds

CITY COLLEGE
NORWICH

This practical book gives you all the ideas you need to make drama a regular and integral part of your school's curriculum, offering detailed suggestions of drama work for ages 4–7. The teaching units are arranged around four strands: drama for literacy; drama and the whole curriculum; drama, film, media and ICT; and drama for performance. The authors provide a wealth of practical activities throughout. Each unit includes:

- explicit links to the *Renewed Framework for literacy* and the wider curriculum;
- a list of resources needed;
- clear learning objectives and outcomes;
- steps for teaching and learning, including how to modify activities to suit your school;
- links to writing;
- assessment guidance.

Based on the authors' experience as teachers and in-service trainers, this book provides a wide range of ideas and activities for inspiring drama across the Foundation Stage and Key Stage 1, and is essential reading for all those interested in bringing drama into their school.

Miles Tandy and **Jo Howell** are advisers with Warwickshire's Educational Development Service, UK. They have written widely about drama and literacy, and their publications include *Creating Writers in the Primary Classroom* (Routledge, 2008) and *Beginning Drama* (Routledge, 2008).

Creating Drama with 4-7 Year Olds

Lesson ideas to integrate drama into the primary curriculum

Miles Tandy and Jo Howell

Routledge
Taylor & Francis Group

LONDON AND NEW YORK

First published 2010
by Routledge
2 Park Square, Milton Park, Abingdon, Oxon OX14 4RN

Simultaneously published in the USA and Canada
by Routledge
270 Madison Ave, New York, NY 10016

Routledge is an imprint of the Taylor & Francis Group, an informa business

Typeset in Goudy and Trade Gothic by Wearset Ltd, Boldon
Printed and bound in Great Britain by TJ International Ltd, Padstow,
Cornwall

British Library Cataloguing in Publication Data
A catalogue record for this book is available from the British Library

Library of Congress Cataloging in Publication Data
Tandy, Miles.
Creating drama with ages 4–7: lesson ideas to integrate drama into the
primary curriculum/Miles Tandy and Jo Howell.
p. cm.
1. Drama in education. 2. Drama–Study and teaching (Primary) 3.
Interdisciplinary approach in education. 4. Education, Primary–Curricula.
I. Howell, Jo., 1972- II. Title.
PN3171.T36 2010
372.66–dc22   2009022558

ISBN10: 0-415-56258-9 (hbk)
ISBN10: 0-415-48349-2 (pbk)
ISBN10: 0-203-86435-2 (ebk)

ISBN13: 978-0-415-56258-4 (hbk)
ISBN13: 978-0-415-48349-0 (pbk)
ISBN13: 978-0-415-86435-7 (ebk)

For Christa Tennant 1949–2005

Contents

Contents

Acknowledgements

Our sincere thanks are due to all those teachers and their classes who have helped develop these materials: those who have lent us their classes; those who have tried some units out; those who have read drafts and made suggestions and comments. Also to all our friends and colleagues at the Educational Development Service for their support, professionalism and friendship. Thanks also to members of the education department of the Royal Shakespeare Company, particularly Mary Johnson, Rachel Gartside and Jacqui O'Hanlon, all of whom have had a profound and lasting effect on our work. Finally, thanks and love to Denise and Gideon for their support and patience throughout.

How to use this book

Recent years have seen a growing interest in the place of drama in the primary school. Many of the teachers with whom we work recognise drama as a very powerful way of engaging children in learning right across the curriculum. Rooted as it is in children's innate capacity to play – to be other people (or other living creatures) at other times and in other places – drama offers a very natural and accessible medium through which children can experience, explore and present ideas. With skilful and sensitive teaching, children can cheerfully tackle ideas and concepts in drama that they might find much more difficult through talking and writing alone. And perhaps most important of all, drama can offer children some of the most engaging, rewarding and joyful experiences that they can have together in their primary schools.

Although many of the teachers with whom we work would share these sentiments entirely, many also tell us that sustaining drama teaching over a whole school year is challenging to say the least. Teaching drama often requires levels of skill and confidence that go well beyond those which most teachers have been given in their initial training. Even if you have been lucky enough to receive some in-service training in teaching drama, you may have found it difficult to sustain your initial enthusiasm once you have used all the strategies and ideas you were given on your course.

So the purpose of this book is twofold: to provide you with plenty of ideas for teaching drama across the age range; and to offer you step-by-step guidance for putting them into practice. *Creating Drama with 4–7 Year Olds* gives you and the other teachers in your school a comprehensive programme of drama teaching and learning. You may wish to use it exactly as it is set out in these pages, but it has also been designed to be used flexibly, moving and adapting units to fit with your curriculum, even designing completely new units if you need to.

If you are new to teaching drama with this age range, you may find it helpful to use these units in conjunction with one of the other practical guides we suggest in Appendix 2. Ideally, you may also want to get some good-quality in-service training for you and the rest of your staff. Like many teachers, once you start making drama a regular part of your teaching practice, you won't want to stop. These units have been carefully designed to make sure that you never have to.

The four strands

Year group	Drama and literacy	Drama and the whole curriculum	Drama, film, media and ICT	Drama for performance
Reception	Castles	The cycle shop	Filming a traditional story	A festival of nursery rhymes
Year 1	*A New Home for a Pirate*	*The Steel Teddy Bear*	*Jim and the Beanstalk*	*The King with Dirty Feet*
Year 2	*The Lost Happy Endings*	Light and dark	*The First Snow of Winter*	*A Midsummer Night's Dream*

Figure 1

Figure 1 shows the four units for each year group. These are stranded under the headings of: drama and literacy; drama and the whole curriculum; drama, film, media and ICT; and drama for performance. The strands continue from this book into *Creating Drama with 7–11 Year Olds* to give a cohesive and comprehensive programme right through the primary phase. The strands are inter-related and have been designed so that the understanding from one unit will reinforce the others for that year group.

Strand 1: Drama and literacy

Teaching children to read and write remains, quite rightly, one of the most important purposes of primary education. Drama has a very particular capacity to bring the teaching of literacy to life, giving children imagined experiences that enrich their reading and writing. The renewed *Primary Framework for teaching literacy and mathematics*, which is currently used in most English primary schools, explicitly encourages the inclusion of drama to immerse children in literature and give them experiences that will support their writing. The *Framework* also includes objectives for speaking and listening, including drama. These objectives are included in the drama and literacy strand, but also appear in all the other strands too.

Strand 2: Drama and the whole curriculum

All drama has to be about something, and drawing that content from the curriculum you will be covering anyway can be a very effective way of making best use of the limited time you have available. Drama can also make a unique contribution to bringing curriculum content alive and making it relevant and meaningful for young children. Once you have taught these units, you will find that the structures and strategies you develop can be applied to all sorts of other curriculum content as drama becomes a natural part of teaching and learning in your classroom.

Strand 3: Drama, film, media and ICT

Film, television and computers are all important sources of learning and entertainment for children. Rather than underestimate the potential of these media, or dismiss them as 'sitting in front of a screen', this strand shows how drama can work with them to help children be active, creative agents with such media, making content rather than just consuming it. Because good drama involves children being up on their feet and moving most of the time, it can greatly enrich their engagement with film, media and ICT.

Strand 4: Drama for performance

Children's performances for others in school, for their parents and for other members of the community can be some of the most exciting and rewarding times in the cultural life of the primary school. This strand shows how performances can be integrated into your programme for drama, building on children's ideas and ambitions to create high-quality work of which everyone can feel proud.

How the units are organised

The units follow a common structure from Reception through to Year 2. They are designed so that you can find your way through them quickly and easily, following the ideas exactly as set down where you want to, perhaps picking from them and adapting them as you become more confident. They are organised under the following headings:

Where this unit fits in

In this section you will see how the unit links to the rest of the curriculum and to the other units for the year group. This is designed to help you at the planning stage, so that your work in drama is integrated fully with the rest of your curriculum. If the work is based on a book, film, play or other story, you will also find a concise synopsis of the plot.

Key learning

The first section under this heading sets out the Key learning for drama. These are the objectives specific to drama which will help not only to keep the work focused as you go through the unit, but will also guide the criteria against which you will assess children's work. As the unit progresses, you will also be carrying out informal assessments of where groups and individuals are, so these objectives may need to be adapted and refined as you go.

You will also find learning objectives from the *Primary Framework for teaching literacy*. There will always be at least one of the drama objectives included, but the work in the units also covers some of the objectives for speaking, listening, reading and writing. These are included only where they are likely to form a significant focus in your work.

Resources

This section includes requirements for the space or spaces you will need to work in, including whether they will need to be blacked out, etc. You will also find lists of any other props and items of costume required so that you can put these together before you start. Pens and large sheets of paper are often needed, but are not always specifically listed in the resources section – it is a good idea to have these around at all times.

Steps for teaching and learning

This is the section where you will find detailed instructions for putting the unit into practice. The structures and activities are outlined step-by-step, rather than specifying them lesson-by-lesson. How long you spend in an individual lesson will vary from school to school, perhaps from one class to another. Even your own lessons may vary in length according to how much time you can make available, the stage the work is at and the particular needs of the children. Some teachers will want to undertake the work quite intensively, perhaps over a few days or a week or two. Others may want to fit the unit into a term or half-term of weekly drama lessons – there is no fixed way in which the units must be taught. You will need to integrate them with whatever planning systems your school has in place, but it is always good to keep in mind that the quality of the children's work matters much more than the paperwork. Photocopying and annotating the unit may be all you need to do.

Although the steps for teaching and learning are clearly set out, the exact course the work takes will depend very much on decisions that you and the children take as the unit progresses. This is particularly true of the performance units where what is offered is more a structure for devising work with children, rather than an exact recipe for the eventual product. There are no ready-made scripts because the intention is that you and they will devise them together as you go. Although the unit on *A Midsummer Night's Dream*, for example, might be done each year, the approach taken and the form of the final performance may vary considerably from one year to the next.

You will find that the units refer to a number of dramatic structures and conventions. The more drama you do in school, the more these will become part of the language that both teachers and children use to plan and talk about their work. A full list of these strategies, with a brief explanation of each, is included in Appendix 1.

Guidance on assessment

With all the detailed assessment you need to carry out in other areas of the primary curriculum, it can be very difficult to make assessing drama a priority. However, if you want to value drama and give it the status it deserves, you need to be able to give as clear an account as possible of what children have learned and how they are progressing. The objectives set out under the 'Key learning for drama' heading will guide your observation, assessment and recording of children's work. In this section, you will find the objectives listed again, along with some prompt questions for each to focus your assessment. You are very unlikely to want to record detailed answers to these questions for all the children, but you may want to record something about those that performed very well during the work, and/or those who found it difficult to engage. But we have deliberately not included complex assessment and recording processes or burdensome paperwork. Your school will already have its own assessment policy and practice in place: the intention of the guidance in this section is to help you gather the information that you will need to fulfil your school's requirements.

Linking to writing

All teachers will be familiar with the complaint, 'I don't know what to write about!' Because good drama immerses children in deep and rich imagined experiences, it can provide a fabulous stimulus for writing. Children will often use richer and more complex language in drama and role play than they might in their everyday talk, so it can have a very significant impact not just on what they write about, but also on the language they use. It is important to stress, though, that this rich language needs to be 'caught' and recorded *at the time*. All too often, children will be full of rich language and exciting ideas as they leave their drama lesson, only for those ideas and language to have evaporated when they settle down to do some writing. This is why we make the links with writing explicit, and suggest that you keep large pens and sheets of paper to hand all the time. A few moments spent recording ideas not only gives you a valuable resource to use back in the classroom, it can also provide a quick and energising change in activity during your lessons.

Adapting this unit

As we have already suggested, the units in this book can be taught exactly as they are set out to provide a comprehensive programme for drama. However, you may find that they do not fit exactly with your other curriculum plans and that you need to make some adjustments to meet your school's needs.

Moving a unit from one year to another should present you with relatively few problems. You will need to look at the objectives and adjust them for a different age group, but the other units should help you do that. There may also be some changes in the steps for teaching and learning to make the activities appropriate for the new age group.

In this section we also give some guidance should you want to adapt the unit for different content: another book may be integral to your plans for literacy, for example, or your other curriculum plans may specify different coverage. The more confident you become with teaching drama, the easier these adjustments and adaptations will become. As you and the rest of the staff become more experienced and confident, you will probably find that you can use the skills and experience you have developed from working your way through these units to devise and teach units of your own.

Above all, the intention is that the units we offer here should allow your drama curriculum to get off to an exciting and practical start. Once drama has become a natural and everyday part of the way you all work, you will find that the units grow into a curriculum that is truly your own and that genuinely meets the needs of the children that you teach.

RL | Castles

Where this unit fits in

Work on castles in the Foundation Stage offers an engaging blend of fiction and factual work. For children of this age, castles can be very exciting places to visit and explore and, if you have one reasonably near your school, a visit would be very worthwhile at the start of this unit. Walking around the walls, peering into the darkest corners, or perhaps seeing some live displays of archery or falconry, can all help to fire children's imaginations and help them to create stories of knights and dragons, lords and ladies, banquets, jesters and tumblers.

Many traditional stories like *Jack and the Beanstalk*, *The Frog Prince* or *The Sleeping Beauty* are set in or around castles. Reading, telling and acting out these stories can help to stimulate children's ideas for imaginative and inventive role play which, in turn, can develop into more structured drama.

The activities outlined in this unit will all offer good drama experiences in themselves. Just as important, though, are the ways in which they will focus, stimulate and extend children's own play which will happen outside any planned drama time.

This unit is likely to form part of a wider focus on castles covering all the Areas of Learning. It will offer plenty of opportunities for including outdoor play, building walls and bridges, practising sword play (safely!) and experimenting with ideas like battering rams. A sand tray will enable exploration of castle mounds and moats, and well-resourced small world play can encourage children to explore the mechanics of a drawbridge or a portcullis.

Key learning

Key learning for drama

By the end of this unit, the children will have:

- invented and played a game together, sticking to its rules and structures;
- contributed their ideas to the developing story;
- enacted the story through sustained action using appropriate language;
- responded to teacher in role.

Primary Framework for literacy objectives

- Creating and shaping texts – attempt writing for various purposes, using features of different forms such as lists, stories and instructions.
- Speaking – use language to imagine and recreate roles and experiences.
- Listening and responding – listen with enjoyment and respond to stories.
- Group discussion, interaction – interact with others, negotiating plans and activities and taking turns in conversation.
- Drama – use language to imagine and recreate roles and experiences.

Resources

- Plenty of cloaks, tabards, etc., of different sizes and textures.
- A range of cardboard boxes, rolls and tubes (including large cardboard rolls from carpets) that can be painted and used to make sections of castle wall, etc.
- An arrow that you have prepared with a note attached as detailed in Step 3.
- 'Dragon footprints' for Step 4.
- A homemade book *How to Catch Dragons* as detailed in Step 5.

Steps for teaching and learning

Step 1: Everyday life in the castle

Once the children have had the opportunity to look at books about castles, perhaps have been on their visit, and maybe looked at some short extracts of video, talk to them about the things that had to be done in and around the castle every day. Make a list of four or five jobs, based on their ideas. For example, these might include:

- winding water from the well;
- sword or archery practice;
- patrolling the walls;
- roasting the meat;
- sweeping the floor.

For each of these ideas, develop an action that the children can easily remember. Then use these actions to play a version of the game 'Captain's Coming'. The teacher calls out one of the jobs and the children do the action until she changes the job. Then you can add in the instruction 'Here comes the King!' (or Queen) at which the children all have to make and hold an exaggerated bow.

Step 2: Making a banquet

Drawing again on what they have learned from books, video and their visit, ask the children what they think a banquet in the castle might have been like. Who would have been there? How might they have dressed? What would they have eaten? What entertainment would there have been? Children can then work in twos and threes to practise for the banquet – some could prepare food and practise serving it, others practise songs to sing and music to play, others the tumbles and jokes of the jesters. You might want to arrange some tables in long rows, with the King and Queen at the head, then narrate what happens at the banquet as the children act it out.

Step 3: A message arrives

Narrate that the banquet was going very well, that everyone was having a wonderful time, and that the King and Queen were delighted with all the work that had gone into it. Then narrate that just as the banquet was about to finish, something very strange happened: an arrow flew through one of the windows and landed in the table right in front of the King and Queen. Holding the arrow, move it through the air and put it on the table in front of the King and Queen. Then narrate that the King and Queen noticed that the arrow had a note attached to it. Ask the King and Queen to untie the message and (if appropriate) read what it says:

> Please help me
> I have been captured by a dragon
> I am in his cave
> I am afraid he will eat me
> Please, please help …

Talk to the children about the note and what it says. Who do they think sent it? Where has it come from? How could they help? As they talk, note down as many of their ideas as you can to use in the next stage of the drama. The next stage of the story is probably best left for the next day so that you can prepare it.

Step 4: Going on a dragon hunt

There are several ways in which you might make some dragon footprints. You could cut them out of paper and lay them on the floor, make one pair out of card and then use them as templates to draw with chalk on the playground, or you could even find a way of printing them in the ground if it is soft enough. As a first stage you may want to go on the dragon hunt all together, but children will also want to go on hunts of their own as their play develops. This will give you very valuable opportunities to listen to and capture their ideas for where the dragon lives and how it behaves.

Step 5: The damaged book

Carefully prepare a book that has the title *How to Catch Dragons*. It needs to look old, worn and tatty. Inside, the pages are missing: there could be signs that they have been torn out, perhaps that they got wet, or you may even go to the trouble of creating some scorched edges of pages suggesting that they have been burned. The book can be left in the role-play area for the children to discover as they come in. They are very likely to bring it to you and you can then talk with them about what it is and what might have happened to the pages. Then you can ask if the children have any idea what the pages might have said before they got damaged. Anyone who works with children of this age will know that they are very unlikely to say they don't know! Depending on the experience and ability of the children you are working with, they may want to re-write the missing pages themselves. This can be particularly effective if only parts of the pages are damaged and their task is to fill in the missing bits. Alternatively, they might get an adult to scribe their ideas and they can add illustrations and diagrams. What is most important is that you finish up with a book that is full of all their imaginative and inventive ideas about catching dragons, because these will inform the next stage of the drama.

Step 6: Catching the dragon

Using as many of the children's ideas as you can, narrate the story of the dragon hunt as the children act it out. At this stage it can be very useful to have something like a 'story stick' which allows you to manage the action. Tell the children that when you tap the stick on the ground three times the story will come alive and they will be the knights that are hunting the dragon, but that if you hold the stick up and call 'story stick!' they must immediately be still. This allows you to comment on what the knights are doing and to praise their remarkable hunting skills.

Step 7: Bringing the dragon home

Naturally enough, the children will probably want to slay the dragon when they catch it – after all, this is what happens in plenty of stories. But if you are prepared to take the role of the dragon yourself, you can use it to challenge and extend their thinking further. For example, you might tell them that you mean the princess no harm, but that you brought her to your cave because you wanted someone to be your friend. You can explain that dragons often find it difficult to find friends because there are so few dragons left after so many have been hunted by brave knights. It can also be difficult to find friends because you are so big and have rather unfortunate habits like breathing fire. At this stage you need to be led by the children, but they may well offer to help, either by being your friends and taking you back to the castle, or by helping you to find friends of your own. Whatever they say, you need to be prepared to follow their ideas and guide the story accordingly. But the story is very likely to develop in ways that allow you to explore themes such as friendship, living together and conservation.

Step 8: A banquet to celebrate

This can be a lovely way of rounding off a topic like this. The knights in the castle might, for example, plan a banquet to celebrate their new friendship and peaceful co-existence with the dragons. They already know some things about banquets from Step 2, but this time you might organise some real food and drink and let them organise dancing and other entertainment. Parents, governors and other members of the community might even be invited along to join in the celebration.

Guidance on assessment

Any assessment of this work will be related back to the Key learning for drama, which stated that by the end of this unit the children will have:

- invented and played a game together, sticking to its rules and structures – *did they all do this? Who contributed ideas?*
- contributed their ideas to the developing story – *who gave their ideas freely? Who engaged in role play beyond the planned drama and brought ideas from that?*
- enacted the story through sustained action using appropriate language – *how well did they stay focused on the story as you were telling it and they were acting it out? Who changed/varied the language they used so that it was appropriate to the castle/dragon hunt?*
- responded to teacher in role – *when you took the role of the dragon, did they listen to what you said, questioning and responding appropriately?*

Adapting this unit

This unit is deliberately structured to fit in with the best Foundation Stage practice and organisation. However, all the drama ideas will work just as readily into Years 1 and 2. If you use them with these age groups you may want to extend the writing activities (for example by expecting a longer and more detailed version of the *How to Catch Dragons* book). You can also extend it by using texts like:

- *Herb, The Vegetarian Dragon*, Julie Bass and Debbie Harter, Barefoot Books, ISBN 1-905-236-47-6, or
- *George and the Dragon*, Chris Wormell, Red Fox, ISBN 976-1-862-30213-6.

RC The cycle shop

Where this unit fits in

Exciting and engaging role-play areas are essential elements of good early-years provision. They allow strong links between the early-years setting and the world outside, and encourage children to adopt adult roles and the language, skills and knowledge associated with them. Shops have always been a popular choice, offering plenty of opportunities for exchanges between shopkeepers and customers, handling money, using telephones, computers and other ICT, and writing orders and messages.

A cycle shop is not an obvious choice, but it offers plenty of rich opportunities not just for buying and selling bikes, but for servicing and repairing them, for giving advice to customers, even for organising charity cycle rides and other local events. It is a very rich environment for exploring the basic technology of bicycles, for thinking about the environmental and health benefits of cycling, and for developing a range of language and communication skills.

This role-play area could be part of a focus on travel and transport which includes all the Areas of Learning. Although it starts with the development of the role-play area, this quickly grows to include a range of outdoor play, and plenty of opportunities to work with parents and the wider community.

Key learning

Key learning for drama

By the end of this unit, the children will have:

- contributed to the development of a role-play cycle shop;
- taken part in a range of role play in the shop, using appropriate language;
- engaged in role play extending beyond the classroom, exploring the roles of mechanic and customer;
- worked together to create a story about an imagined local issue.

Primary Framework for literacy objectives

- Speaking – enjoy listening to and using spoken and written language and readily turn to it in play and learning; use language to imagine and recreate roles and experiences.
- Creating and shaping texts – attempt writing for various purposes, using features of different forms such as lists and instructions.
- Group discussion, interaction – interact with others, negotiating plans and activities and taking turns in conversation; use talk to organise, sequence and clarify thinking, ideas, feelings and events.
- Drama – use language to imagine and recreate roles and experiences.

Resources

- Bicycles, tricycles and a selection of spare parts.
- Cycle helmets, reflective jackets, overalls and other appropriate clothing.
- Tools (pumps, spanners, screwdrivers, etc.) that you know the children can use safely.
- A till, card reader, etc.
- A computer.
- Plenty of paper, books for recording repairs and orders, etc.
- Bike catalogues, brochures, etc.
- Phone/mobile phones.
- Simple walkie-talkie devices (optional).

Steps for teaching and learning

Step 1: Setting up the role-play area

The best role-play areas are set up in negotiation with the children. A good place to start is by asking who has a bike. Then discuss how they got them – were some given as presents? Did anyone go to a bike shop to get theirs? How did they choose? How did they know which was the right sort of bike for them? Did they buy a cycle helmet at the same time? Who has a bike that they have grown out of? Children will have lots to say in response to these questions to really set them thinking about bikes, bike shops and the sorts of things they might like in theirs.

It is a really good idea to inform parents and carers about your plans at a very early stage. Ask if anyone has old bikes that they no longer use and could lend for the shop. Second-hand bikes have relatively little value these days and are often thrown away and could be reclaimed from your local recycling centre. If parents or others do offer to lend them, it might be an idea politely to ask them to clean them thoroughly first. Not only will this make it much safer for the children to handle them, but everything being shiny and bright is a very important part of the look of a bike shop. Some of the bikes may be taken apart (with their owner's permission!) and used to build a collection of spare parts because you are unlikely to be able to accommodate many complete bicycles. You will quickly find that you have plenty to put on display. Depending on what space is available, it can be good to locate the bike shop near the outdoor area as many shops have bikes displayed outside as well as in. Setting the outdoor display up with prices and special offers can be just as important a daily job in your role-play area as it is in any bike shop.

You are likely to want a counter with a till, and a workshop area behind it where bikes can be repaired. Add in a good variety of posters, leaflets and brochures, some commercially produced and some the children have made for themselves, and your bike shop will soon start to come to life.

Step 2: Visiting a local shop

There are a surprising number of small, local cycle shops still operating. If you have one that is reasonably close by, it is well worth making contact. A quick visit will give you lots more ideas for developing the shop in your classroom. They may be prepared to give you old catalogues and brochures for your shop and perhaps some empty boxes for spare parts, cycle helmets, etc. You may be able to arrange a visit for some or all of the children. If not, take a digital camera with you and ask if it is OK to take some pictures to help the children with their ideas. Most local traders are more than happy to help, particularly if it might encourage children and their parents through the door.

Step 3: Repairs and advice

Many children will readily take the roles of shopkeepers, mechanics and customers and play with integrity and purpose. But if adults are also prepared to take these roles they can help to give the role-play area status, extending and challenging the children's play. What matters is that they do this with absolute integrity. Try taking a bike into the shop with a simple problem – it need be no more than a tyre that needs pumping up. If you talk naturally to the shopkeeper or mechanic about it, you will get a very valuable opportunity to hear how they use language and status in a relationship that is different from the usual adult/child.

Step 4: Writing and recording

All the bikes sold in the shop will need a receipt and probably a guarantee. It is also very easy to design simple forms and log books where repairs and sales can be recorded. They need only headings like 'Customer name', 'Date', 'Repairs needed' and 'When collected'. What matters is that they make writing an integral and natural part of the role play. If you have a computer set up in the shop, you can send emails asking for details of products, prices or perhaps advice on equipment or repairs. The bikes could also be issued with safety certificates which would entail designing not only the certificates themselves, but also checklists and procedures for carrying out the checks. Clipboards and pens/pencils will quickly become part of everyday life in the shop.

Step 5: Moving outdoors

As we have already suggested, like many bike shops yours could have a display outside the shop, and there are plenty of other opportunities for extending the play outdoors. Bikes will need to be 'road tested' by customers wanting to buy them or by mechanics checking repairs, so you might want to designate a part of the playground for this. You could also set up a course with obstacles, challenges and road signs where customers could learn to cycle more safely. Depending on how much room you have got in your grounds, you may also set up a cycle trail. Many children will have been on these with their families and can help to suggest signage, stopping places and points of interest.

Step 6: The bicycle ambulance

We encountered one of these in Cambridge, a city where cycling is enduringly popular. Setting up a repair tricycle, perhaps with a small trailer for tools, will open up all sorts of extensions to the outdoor play. Customers whose bicycles have broken down can phone (or perhaps text) the shop and ask for help and the cycle repairer can ride to their assistance. The repairer can keep in touch with the shop via a simple walkie-talkie radio, checking for directions and reporting back on progress. Back at the shop, a careful log needs to be kept, detailing the customer's name, time of call, location, nature of problem, etc. The shop may even have a board displaying letters of thanks from grateful customers.

Step 7: The cycle trail

The possibility of a cycle trail was suggested in Step 5. It will offer plenty of opportunities for making information leaflets and maps to go with it so that it can be promoted in the shop. Once the trail is established and it is being used in the children's play, you can introduce the idea that it is under threat in some way. Come into the shop as a customer who has heard that there are plans to build a new road right along the path of the cycle trail. Have the people in the shop heard about it, and what do they think should be done about it? This can encourage children to make posters, write letters and invite people in the shop to sign a petition to keep the trail open – all good ways of showing how writing can help to change things for the better. Since this is a fictional road and a fictional campaign to prevent it, you can make absolutely certain that the children are successful!

Step 8: The charity cycle ride

Through the shop, you and the children could organise a version of a charity cycle ride. Children can design and make posters to advertise it, and sponsorship forms for those taking part. They need only complete a few laps of the playground, but it would be a lovely event to which they could invite parents, carers, governors and members of the community. It would make a delightful way of rounding off the project and celebrating what the children have achieved together.

Guidance on assessment

Any assessment of this work will be related back to the Key learning for drama, which stated that by the end of this unit the children will have:

- contributed to the development of a role-play cycle shop – *who contributes ideas? Who comes up with original and inventive suggestions?*
- taken part in a range of role play in the shop, using appropriate language – *if you take part in this role play with them, you will get fabulous insights into their use of language. Many children use much more sophisticated language in role play than they do at other times.*

- engaged in role play extending beyond the classroom, exploring the roles of mechanic and customer – *you will get most insight here when they are working with the bike ambulance. If you can get hold of the walkie-talkie, listening in on their conversations will give you plenty of assessment opportunities.*
- worked together to create a story about an imagined local issue – *how do they react when you go into the shop and tell them about the new road? Who offers to help? What ideas do they have?*

Adapting this unit

The work outlined here is designed to complement the best Foundation Stage practice. But elements of it could certainly be adapted for Years 1 and 2. Many classrooms for these age groups now include role-play areas and this one would work very well. You are likely to want to extend the reading and writing aspects of the work, and probably look at some of the other issues (for example, the threat to the cycle trail) through more formally structured drama.

RF Filming a traditional story

Where this unit fits in

Traditional stories are likely to form an important part of the curriculum in the Foundation Stage. There will be significant variations in the stories children have been read and told when they enter school, but well-known stories such as *Goldilocks and the Three Bears*, *Little Red Riding Hood* or *Jack and the Beanstalk* quickly become part of the shared culture in many Reception classes. It is important that these stories are shared in as many ways as possible. They might be read aloud in a number of versions, told by the teacher and/or other adults, re-told by the children using props and toys, and acted out using props and costumes in the role-play area.

This unit takes advantage of the increasing availability of digital video in primary schools. Even if you do not have access to some of the digital video cameras and editing software that have been specifically developed for children, you may find that digital cameras that you have in and around school can take video clips and you can assemble and edit them using software that is freely available.

Making a film like this with children of this age group is a very rewarding way of developing and celebrating their knowledge of traditional stories. It will also present them with a range of creative challenges in thinking about how they will best tell the story through the camera.

This unit might connect to a larger unit of work you have planned on traditional stories that embraces several Areas of Learning. It may also link with other work you are doing with ICT. Many of the cameras that are now available can be readily used by children in this age group and many include very straightforward editing software that they will quickly learn to use.

Key learning

Key learning for drama

By the end of this unit, the children will have:

- explored and represented a number of traditional stories through movement, voice and sound;
- used props and costumes to enhance and clarify their storytelling;
- identified the main points of a story and placed them in sequence;
- reflected on their own and others' work, suggesting improvements as appropriate.

Primary Framework for literacy objectives

- Speaking – use talk to organise, sequence and clarify thinking, ideas, feelings and events.
- Listening and responding – listen with enjoyment and respond to stories.
- Group discussion, interaction – use talk to organise, sequence and clarify thinking, ideas, feelings and events.
- Drama – use language to imagine and recreate roles and experiences.
- Understand and interpret texts – retell narratives in the correct sequence, drawing on the language patterns of stories.

Resources

- A camera that will take digital video clips. You may have access to some of the cameras that are made specifically for children to use (for example the Digital Blue digital movie creator or the Tuff-Cam). But this unit could also be undertaken with any digital camera that takes video clips, although children may need more assistance from an adult to use them.
- Editing software. The cameras that are made specifically for children generally come with their own editing software. Otherwise editing software such as Windows Movie Maker is widely available on most computers and will readily import files from most cameras.
- A range of props and costumes. You will probably have many of these in your classroom already, and they can be added to as you go, depending on the story the children have chosen to film.
- An interactive whiteboard. This is by no means essential, but it will be very useful at the editing stage as well as giving a really good way for children to share their finished work.

Much of the filming may be done using the role-play area as the setting, but you will also want to encourage children to be as imaginative as possible about the places they choose to film their work. Most cameras work best with as much light as possible, so any filming that can be done outside will not only give better final results, but will also encourage children to be more imaginative in how they create their settings.

A unit of work like this can be very frustrating if the technology lets you down. It is even more frustrating and disappointing for the children if you have told them they are going to make a film and the project is not completed. So it is well worth taking time to familiarise yourself with the hardware and software that you will be using before you start. It is also a very good idea to talk to your school's ICT co-ordinator about the project and make use of their expertise throughout. You may also find there are parents and/or other members of the community who have used some of the technology before and are willing to help: they may, of course, need some careful managing to make sure the finished product is the children's own work! Always have plenty of spare batteries and, if possible, a spare camera or two to hand – once children start work, you want as little as possible to get in their way.

Steps for teaching and learning

Step 1: Collecting and sharing stories

You will probably be reading, telling and sharing traditional stories as part of your daily routine. A good way to start this project is to set up and start to fill a 'story chest'. An old wooden chest would be great, but many of the large toy retailers or educational suppliers provide chests and boxes that will do perfectly well. Encourage the children to bring in anything they have that will help you tell traditional stories. This may include books they have at home, video and DVD versions of stories, or story tapes and CDs. They may also have puppets, toys and other props that relate to the stories you have been sharing – three wooden bowls for the Three Bears, for example. If you have access to a digital voice recorder, you may also want to send it home with children so that their parents, grandparents or other friends and family can record a reading or, better still, an oral re-telling of a traditional story they remember. The story chest will soon be full to the brim and serve to remind everyone of the impressive range of stories they share.

Step 2: Setting up the role-play area

Talk to the children about how they would like to set up their role-play area. They may decide to base it on one particular story and develop it as, for example, the Three Bears' cottage or the Giant's castle from *Jack and the Beanstalk*. Or they may decide that they want it to be somewhere where lots of traditional stories can be acted out and explored, so you may want to set it up as a cottage or perhaps a wood that could be in all sorts of stories. The props and costumes from the story chest will be very useful.

Step 3: Guess the story

This can be a great game to play together as a class when you have a spare moment. Invite individual or pairs of children to choose props and/or costumes from the story chest. Very quickly they must use the props/costumes to mime a moment from a story that everyone knows and see how quickly the rest of the class can guess what it is. It may also be a really good time to introduce the camera(s) you will be using for the filming project. Either you or one of the children can film the mime so that it can be shown again at a later time. When you show the clip, it is a really good opportunity to talk about what made it easy or difficult to guess the story. This will get children thinking about what works well when telling stories through film, and help them in their later work.

Step 4: A story in three pictures

This will work best if children are in groups of two, three or four. The challenge is to tell a traditional story in three pictures which they make using themselves (tableaux). They can be either still pictures or short pieces of movement/mime. The teacher calls out the numbers 'one', 'two', 'three', and the children show their pictures in order. Depending on where and how you have organised this game, you, another adult, or another group of children can see how quickly they can guess what the story is and what each picture shows.

Step 5: Introducing the camera(s)

As any Reception teacher will know only too well, children will not sit for long while you explain how to use the cameras. You may find it easier to show children in small groups, or perhaps get a teaching assistant to do so. Once they have been shown, it is important that the camera is as freely available as possible so that they can practise and become familiar with it. A good way of doing this might be to combine it with the role-play area and designate a child as 'camera person' to film some of the play that happens. If you have an interactive whiteboard, the film clips can be shared either with the group or the whole class at the end of a session.

Step 6: Choosing the story

By now the children will have lots of experience of traditional stories and should have plenty to choose from. They should also be getting familiar not only with how the camera works, but also getting more used to being in front of it and seeing themselves on screen.

You will now need to decide whether you want to make one film, with different pairs and groups contributing different bits of the story, or whether you want to film a number of stories, with a different group taking responsibility for each. This decision will obviously depend on the time you have available, but it will also be influenced by how readily the children have taken to the cameras and how much adult support you are able to give them.

Step 7: What shall they film first?

Having chosen their story, the children will quickly want to make a start. It is probably best to film the story in chronological order to begin with, although it is also important to realise that you can add clips of film in later as well if you think you have missed something out.

At this stage you can show the children how to create a simple storyboard. This is a device used by many film-makers to plan what they will film, where and when. Ask the children which bits of the story will need filming and record each of their ideas on a separate sheet of paper as a drawing (very simple stick people drawings are all you need), perhaps adding a few words to remind everyone what the scene will be. If, for example, the children are filming *Goldilocks and the Three Bears*, they may decide that their scenes will be:

- The Bears wake up.
- The Bears eat their porridge but it is too hot.

- The Bears go for a walk.
- Goldilocks comes to the house.
- The Bears come home.
- Who's been eating my porridge?
- Who's been sitting in my chair?
- Who's been sleeping in my bed?
- The Bears chase Goldilocks away.

This structure represents the story at its very simplest and each of the scenes may require more than one camera shot. The simple storyboard of pieces of paper can be pinned to the wall and moved around to check you have everything in the right order.

Step 8: Imaginative settings

Encourage the children to think about the places around school where each of the scenes could be filmed. Some may be filmed in the role-play area, but others might be better using other locations around the school. A few trees and bushes, for example, can readily be made to look like a forest if children are selective about where they point the camera.

Step 9: Introducing editing

How far you decide to involve the children in the editing of their own work will depend partly on how confident you feel with the technology, but also on the kind of editing software you have available. Some of the cameras that have been developed especially for children have their own very simple editing software which children at this age can pick up very quickly. Most just have a library of the children's clips which have been downloaded from the camera and a storyboard at the bottom of the screen. They need only to drag the clips onto the storyboard in the order in which they want them in their film. Most software also includes a feature that allows them to trim the beginnings and ends of clips to get rid of any unwanted film – for example where they have inadvertently filmed a child saying 'What now?' at the beginning of a clip which is otherwise fine. These 'drag and drop' and 'trim' features should be all you and they need to put a simple film together of which you will all be proud.

If you want to add more sophisticated features like titles and music, there is no reason why you should not do this later, perhaps with the support of your ICT co-ordinator. The children will have the opportunity to learn much more about editing themselves as they move through the school.

Step 10: Sharing your films

Once children have made something like a film, they are generally bursting to share it with others. You may be able to show your film to the whole school as part of an assembly. You may also want to invite parents and other members of the community in to see your film(s), maybe as part of a bigger celebration/performance based on all the work you have done on stories.

At this stage you might also consider setting up a role-play area as a cinema. Children can put together a programme saying which films will be shown at which times, make tickets and posters, show people to their seats, even sell ice creams and popcorn. And, as you will know very well, they will not tire of seeing and showing their films over and over again!

Guidance on assessment

Any assessment of this work will be related back to the Key learning for drama, which stated that by the end of this unit the children will have:

* explored and represented a number of traditional stories through movement, voice and sound – *much of this work will give you valuable opportunities to observe how well children have listened to and understood the stories you have been sharing, and how readily and confidently they perform them for themselves and others.*

- used props and costumes to enhance and clarify their storytelling – *do they choose props and costumes just because they like them, or can they also say how they will help to tell the story more clearly?*
- identified the main points of a story and placed them in sequence – *could they identify the most important parts of the story to film and put them (or help you put them) in the right order?*
- reflected on their own and others' work, suggesting improvements as appropriate – *were they willing to re-take film clips if they weren't happy with them? Did they notice if, for example, a car drove past the Three Bears wood while they were filming?*

Linking to writing

There are plenty of writing opportunities that arise from this work, including:

- storyboards and other notes/drawings to help in their filming;
- posters, adverts and programmes for the cinema;
- all sorts of text for the cinema foyer and shop.

Adapting this unit

Digital video cameras and editing software are fast becoming a natural and everyday part of many children's lives, both at home and at school. This unit is just one example of how they can learn from the earliest age to use this technology creatively and imaginatively. As they grow familiar and confident with it, they can use it to record all sorts of aspects of their work. The basic structure of this unit – familiarisation with content, planning and filming together, editing and sharing – could be applied to all sorts of content.

A festival of nursery rhymes

Where this unit fits in

Many children have a repertoire of songs, stories and rhymes that they know by the time they start school. These may have been passed on by parents, grandparents or other family and friends. They may also know them from books, CDs, DVDs and television programmes. There will, of course, be wide variations in who knows what and some children may know very few. By building and celebrating a shared collection as part of this unit, children will build up a deep knowledge of stories, songs and rhymes that can amuse, intrigue and entertain. As well as their intrinsic value, these traditional songs and rhymes can make a huge contribution to children's language development.

This unit might work very well in the autumn term as a way of reinforcing connections between home, school and the community. It might also work very well as a project for the summer term, perhaps culminating in a performance for an audience that includes not only the children's own parents and family, but also those of children who will be starting school in the next academic year.

As with all the Reception units, this is likely to be part of a wider focus (in this case, on traditional stories and rhymes) which will include all the Areas of Learning. It is also a really good opportunity to involve the community, not only in the final performance, but also in gathering a very local collection of stories and rhymes that help celebrate what they share and who they are.

Key learning

Key learning for drama

By the end of this unit, the children will have:

- collected, explored and represented a number of nursery rhymes through movement, voice and sound;
- made choices about their performance based on their own preferences;
- refined their performances, taking account of audience;
- reflected on their own and others' work, suggesting improvements as appropriate.

Primary Framework for literacy objectives

- Speaking – use talk to organise, sequence and clarify thinking, ideas, feelings and events; enjoy listening to and using spoken and written language and readily turn to it in play and learning; speak clearly and audibly with confidence and control and show awareness of the listener.
- Listening and responding – listen with enjoyment and respond to stories, songs and other music, rhymes and poems, and make up their own stories, songs, rhymes and poems.
- Group discussion, interaction – interact with others, negotiating plans and activities.
- Drama – use language to imagine and recreate roles and experiences.
- Engaging with and responding to texts – listen with enjoyment to stories, songs, rhymes and poems, sustain attentive listening and respond with relevant comments, questions and actions.

Resources

- A good selection of costumes and props associated with rhymes you collect – obviously this collection will need to build as the stories, songs and rhymes do.
- A 'stage' area somewhere in the classroom or perhaps outdoors – this will be used by children when they are playing with and developing ideas and rehearsing for the eventual performance.
- A good space for performance – this may be the school hall, but it might also be outdoors, or perhaps in a local community hall.
- A 'story chest' to collect stories, songs, rhymes and ideas from children and parents – this may be an old wooden chest or trunk you can get hold of, or perhaps one of the soft, foldable toy chests that are available.
- Good source and reference books such as *The Mother Goose Treasury* by Raymond Briggs, illustrated anthologies such as *Michael Foreman's Nursery Rhymes*, and perhaps some books for your own interest and reference such as *The Oxford Dictionary of Nursery Rhymes* by Iona and Peter Opie.

Steps for teaching and learning

Step 1: Collecting and sharing favourite rhymes

This step can begin with a conversation with the children about the songs and rhymes they know. It will need quite skilful and sensitive handling as many may be unclear what distinguishes nursery rhymes from any other songs and rhymes. You might find it best to begin by singing a few very well-known rhymes like 'Humpty Dumpty', 'Jack and Jill' or 'Little Bo Peep', and then talk about what they have in common. As the children share other songs and rhymes they know, talk about how they know them, who first sung them to them and what stories the songs and rhymes tell. These conversations will allow you to start filling a 'story chest' with the titles of rhymes and songs. If children learned some of theirs from books, CDs and DVDs, these could be added to the chest as well.

Encourage children to talk to their parents, grandparents, friends and other family members about the songs and rhymes they remember from their own childhoods. These could be written down and brought into school, or you might have some simple recording devices that children can take home and ask friends and family to record the songs and rhymes they know. Some of these may be in languages other than English and this can be a great way of raising awareness of other languages in your community and starting to celebrate its cultural diversity.

You will need to monitor what comes in quite carefully and make thoughtful decisions about what is included in the chest. Some rhymes and songs, though sent in with the best intentions, might be inappropriate or even offensive to some groups. Others may be inappropriate for the age range, and others not really fit the theme of traditional rhymes and songs. Use you judgement, but try also to be as inclusive as possible so that people feel that their contributions are valued.

Step 2: Singing, learning and sharing

The times of the day when the whole class is together will offer great opportunities to spend a few minutes looking in the story chest. Pick out a few rhymes and songs that you can all recite or sing together. This will quickly help you to get an idea which ones are the children's favourites: those that amuse and entertain; those they all know well; those with stories that intrigue and interest them. As the work develops, each short session can begin with some songs and rhymes you all know, then perhaps add in a couple of new ones so that a shared repertoire builds over time.

Step 3: Playing with songs, rhymes and stories

Set up a small 'stage' area. This might be a corner of the classroom or perhaps an outside area. It should be somewhere where children can play and experiment with some of the rhymes and songs you have been sharing. This play can be encouraged by putting out a few props associated with a rhyme or song, asking groups of children to see what the props might represent, and then asking them to use them to make a short performance that they can share with the rest of the group. This will help to build up familiarity with the material and develop confidence in performing. Some rhymes, 'Jack and Jill' for example, tell a very simple story which takes only a minute or two to act out. You need only to provide a bucket, some brown paper and a bottle labelled 'Vinegar'. Then leave it to the children's inventiveness and imagination to come up with a way of presenting the song and its story. They are very likely to ask if they can show the rest of the class what they have done. These small incidental sharing times are a great opportunity to start developing a critical awareness of performance. Does the rest of the class like their work? Did they laugh in the right places? Have they got ideas for how they can make it clearer or better? Building an atmosphere of confidence and positive encouragement at this stage will really pay off when children are expected to perform to larger audiences.

Step 4: Making performance choices

As children are given plenty of opportunities to play and experiment, they will become familiar with lots of songs and rhymes, and will soon develop preferences and favourites. This is a really good opportunity to make simple charts or pictograms. By this point you will want to introduce the idea of sharing your performances with mums, dads, friends and families. Which ones do they think they will like best? Which of their performances do they like best? Where would be a good place to put on the performance? Who shall they invite? It is really important to involve children in all these discussions and decisions so that they feel the eventual outcome is very much the result of their own work and ideas. Encourage ambition, imagination and excitement, and then be as inventive and determined as you can in seeing the children's ideas through.

Step 5: Refining and developing performances

Teachers are sometimes put off creating performances with children of this age by long and tiresome 'rehearsals' in the school hall during which they and the children become tired and irritable. Real rehearsals are just as much about inventing performances together as they are about repetitive practising. As much as anything, your job is to look at children's work with an encouraging, questioning and constructively critical eye through which you help them to make their work the best it can be. Sometimes this is about things as apparently simple as being able to hear. The more this can be made into a game the better. If you have a performance space outside, tell the children you're going to see how far away you can go and still be able to hear them. To begin with, this will have them shouting at the tops of voices, but it is often easier to bring it back down from here than it is to get children to 'speak up'. You can use similar games for getting movement and gesture as clear as possible. Whenever you can, involve the children in refining and developing each other's performances. This is a really good early opportunity to develop a language of critical encouragement: 'I really liked that bit because …'

Step 6: Making more choices

By now you might have some 12 or 15 songs and rhymes that have become favourites and which you know you want to include. What order should you put them in? Rather than spend a long time talking about this, have pictures to represent each (perhaps digital photographs of the children performing) and put them on a board or table where children can experiment with different orders, talking in pairs and groups about which ones go best together, which might get them off to the best start, and which will make a good finale. If each piece lasts a couple of minutes or so, you will end up with a show of around 30–45 minutes, which is plenty for children of this age.

Some props and costumes you will already have from the development stage, but others will still need to be added. This is a terrific opportunity to involve parents and the wider community, many of whom will be only too happy to help you find and make what is needed.

Step 7: Audiences and spaces

Talk to the children about who might like to see their show. Their own parents and families are likely to form the main audience, but who else might they like to invite? Are there local nurseries and play groups who might enjoy the show? What about older people in the community who might like hearing some of the songs and rhymes they remember from their own childhoods?

Think carefully about the space(s) in which the performance will happen. How shall you seat your audience so that everyone gets the best chance to see and hear? Might it be better to do three or four performances for small audiences rather than one big one?

Step 8: The final performance

It is really important that the children approach the final performance of their work with confidence and excitement. Attitudes that they form with this project may stay with them for a very long time. What matters most is that the atmosphere on the day is one of joyful celebration of all that you have done together.

If you are going to make posters, programmes and tickets, involve the children in this as much as possible. As much as you can, maintain a sense that you are all responsible for everything that happens and that you should all be very proud of everyone's work. It is very natural for parents to have a particular interest and eye for their own child's work, but if you have developed a really strong sense of collective ensemble and shared work, then they will be helped to see how their child's work is part of a greater whole. And the rapturous applause will say it all!

Guidance on assessment

Any assessment of this work will be related back to the Key learning for drama, which stated that by the end of this unit the children will have:

- collected, explored and represented a number of nursery rhymes through movement, voice and sound – *who has original and inventive ideas? Who is good at bringing out the ideas of others? Who uses their voice clearly and well?*
- made choices about their performance based on their own preferences – *who has strong opinions and gives good reasons?*
- refined their performances, taking account of audience – *who shows that they have thought about this? Who is clearly taking account of their audience and 'playing to them' as they perform?*
- reflected on their own and others' work, suggesting improvements as appropriate – *who could offer good suggestions? Could they keep their observations positive and supportive?*

Adapting this unit

The structure of this unit could be used with other content and ideas taken from your school community. A good example might be collecting the playground songs, games and rhymes that parents, grandparents, friends and people from the wider community remember. This would also make a very good performance project for older children.

1L A New Home for a Pirate

This unit is based on the picture story book *A New Home for a Pirate*, by Ronda Armitage and Holly Swain, Puffin, ISBN 978-0-141-50025-6.

Where this unit fits in

Jed is a pirate, but he doesn't enjoy it. He finds the ship very cramped and he suffers from seasickness. So he tells his family that he is leaving because he wants to live in a house.

His mum and dad help him to pack his 'pirate paraphernalia' and he sets off. As he travels in search of his new home, Jed meets various characters in need of help and each time he uses something from his 'pirate paraphernalia'. Each of the characters he helps also joins him in his search for a new home. The last person he helps is a farmer with a troublesome bull. The farmer says that he is not really a farmer any more and that he would rather be a pirate. The farmer has just the house that Jed wants, so they agree to a swap.

This unit might connect to other work you are doing on pirates – children in this age group will enjoy the traditional image of pirates that is presented through the story, but many will also identify with the character of Jed who wants to do things in his own way. You may also include PSHE work about understanding and accepting difference, helping others and friendship.

Key learning

Key learning for drama

By the end of this unit, the children will have:

- represented parts of the story using sound, voice and movement;
- played a game together, following the rules and making suggestions for how the game can be developed;
- responded appropriately to the teacher in role, keeping in their own roles as they do so;
- used locations, costumes and props imaginatively and inventively;
- collaborated to devise a shared party/celebration using music, song, movement and dance as appropriate.

Primary Framework for literacy objectives

- Listening – retell stories, ordering events using story language.
- Drama – explore familiar themes and characters through improvisation and role play.
- Understanding and interpreting texts – make predictions showing an understanding of ideas, events and characters.
- Engaging with and responding to texts – visualise and comment on events, characters and ideas, making imaginative links to their own experiences.
- Creating and shaping texts – convey information and ideas in simple non-narrative forms.

Resources

Pictures and/or objects that represent Jed's 'pirate paraphernalia', which comprises:

- a long rope;
- a pirate hat;
- pirate underpants;
- great-grandad's wooden leg;

- a parrot (stuffed);
- a cutlass;
- a spotted handkerchief;
- an eye patch;
- pirate pyjamas;
- socks;
- a toothbrush.

Most of these resources can be assembled quite easily and improvised from the bits and pieces you will probably have if this forms part of a larger piece of work on the theme of pirates.

Although many of the teaching ideas in this unit can be used effectively in the classroom, you will also find it helpful to have access to the hall.

Steps for teaching and learning

Step 1: Playing pirates

Pirates seem to be enduringly popular with young children. Although there are plenty of picture story books on the theme, many of the children's ideas about pirates will come from film and television. Setting up the role-play area as a pirate ship and/or a desert island can be very successful and lead to all sorts of reading and writing – instructions for how to find treasure, messages in bottles, etc. Talking to the class about what they already know about pirates is the best way to start, then using the discussion to help them make decisions about how they want to set up the role-play area.

Step 2: The *Pirates* game

Using a suitable space (probably the hall) play the well-known game *Pirates*, in which the teacher calls out instructions that everyone has to follow:

- Port! – everyone moves to the left side of the space.
- Starboard! – everyone to the right.
- Forward! – everyone to the front.
- Aft! – everyone to the back.
- Scrub the decks – everyone kneels down and mimes cleaning the deck.
- Captain's coming! – everyone stands and salutes.

You can adapt this game for this particular story by making the space in which you play it smaller and smaller to show how Jed dislikes life on board the ship because it is so cramped – you just need to mark out the floor with masking tape. Clearly you will need to be aware of the safety issues connected with a game like this and negotiate carefully with the children how you will all play the game together safely. The children can also make suggestions for other commands and actions to go with them which you can then add into the game

Step 3: An active reading of the story

For this activity you will need either pictures of or (much better) the actual items of 'pirate paraphernalia' listed in the resources section of this unit. It is also important that the children have not seen or read the story before this activity.

Divide the children into groups and give each group an object from the list. There are eleven items in the list, but not all are used in the story so you can have anything from four or five to ten groups of children depending on the size of your class. Groups of three or four will probably work best.

Read the story aloud and pause at each point where Jed meets someone in need of help. He meets a bird who lost her nest, a sheep who is caught in brambles, a dog with a broken leg, and a farmer whose bull is loose in the field. When the story is paused, ask the groups to think of a way in which their item might help. Then ask them to represent their idea as either a still picture or a short mime.

Give time for discussion, then count to three and ask the groups to show their pictures/mimes. It is probably best to show them all at the same time rather than go round the groups and see each one in turn. Quickly comment on all the different ideas you can see, wondering aloud which one might be on the next page. Then ask the children to sit down again while you read on. It is very important that you don't allow this to turn into a game of 'Who got it right?', rather you need to talk to the children about the ideas they all had and how the author could just as easily have used one of theirs. In the story, Jed uses his rope to escape the bull, but the group who has got the pirate underpants might, for example, suggest that he puts these over the bull's head (his horns can go through the leg holes!) to help him avoid the bull. The important thing is that children are listening carefully to what is read, then working together in their groups to invent and represent a way in which their object might help.

Step 4: Making new 'pages'

Like many picture story books, *A New Home for a Pirate* has a clear pattern to each of the pages where Jed meets someone in need of help. In their groups, ask the children to think of other people and/or animals that Jed could have encountered on his journey and who Jed could have helped using their item of pirate paraphernalia. Give them time to talk about their ideas in their groups, then ask them to represent them as a short scene – the only rules are that they must show the problem the person/animal has, include Jed saying 'Shiver me timbers! I have the very thing', and show clearly how he helps. With these ideas you will probably want to watch each group's work in turn and talk with the whole class about the ideas and how they were shown in the short scenes.

Step 5: The pirate library

At the end of the story Jed takes Farmer Ted to meet his family. They agree to teach him how to be a pirate and Ted goes to 'pirate school'. A good way of getting children to start thinking about the school and its curriculum is to ask what books they think might be in the school library. This will probably work best if children work in pairs. You will need plenty of scrap paper and some large felt pens. As children come with their ideas for titles in the pirate library, they write (and draw) on the scrap paper to make a very quick version of the book cover. Have an area of the floor to represent the library and ask the children to place their 'book covers' on the floor as they do them – they can do as many as they like. Then you can talk about how the pirate library might be organised and the class can rearrange the titles accordingly.

Next you can ask the children in their pairs to look around the pirate library. Ask each pair to pick up one book they would love to be able to read, then bring the class back together and talk about their choices. Then you can ask each pair to choose a book they would like to write – these titles can be taken and used for a short writing project where the children write and illustrate the books they have chosen.

Step 6: Pirate school

Begin by asking the children what lessons they think might happen at pirate school – they might mention treasure map reading, walking the plank and (almost certainly!) sword or cutlass fighting. In groups, ask them to make still pictures of different times in the pirate day – 9 o'clock, 11 o'clock, 1 o'clock and 3 o'clock. Still images are used here because they can help to control activities like sword fighting, so you will need to insist on the discipline of making them absolutely still, even though you might ask the children to bring them to life later.

When the groups have had time to devise their images, review them all together by calling out the four times of the pirate day – you call '9 o'clock!' and all the groups must make their images to show what the pirates are doing at this time. You may make some brief comments about what the different groups are doing while they hold their images completely still.

Step 7: Ted learns to be a pirate

For this activity the teacher needs to take the role of Ted as he is learning to be a pirate. Ask each group to choose one of their images of pirate school and tell them that they are going to bring it to life so that Ted can join the lesson. You will need to do some careful negotiating here so that you get a good range of lessons to join – otherwise you may learn nothing but cutlass fighting!

Working with each group in turn, and with the other groups watching as you do, ask the children to hold their still image and then on a count of three to bring it to life. When the image has come to life, the teacher walks in and joins it as Ted. You can have great fun with this if you make a point of getting things wrong and ask the pirates to explain very slowly and carefully exactly what you should be doing. They will need to respond in role and it will be a good opportunity for you to see how well they can do this.

Step 8: Postcards home

You can work with the idea that Ted and Jed keep writing to each other once Ted has gone to sea and Jed has settled down on the farm with his friends. In their groups, children can talk about the things that happen and then represent these as more still images. Encourage them to think about where they will put their 'pictures' – outside on a climbing frame may be a good place to look like part of a ship for instance – and what they will wear and use as props. These pictures can then be captured with a digital camera and printed off to make postcards for the children to add their writing. Each of these postcards will describe a new incident and development of the story.

Step 9: The pirate party

This is an enjoyable way of bringing all the work together and celebrating it at the end of the unit. In role as Jed, the teacher can tell the children that all his family and Farmer Ted are coming to stay for a few days and that he wants to give them the best pirate party ever. What sort of food should they have? What songs could they sing together? Do the children know any pirate dances? What sort of games do pirates like to play?

Once the children have helped you to plan the party, take an afternoon to put all their ideas into practice with them. You could ask another class, or perhaps parents and younger siblings, to come along and join you. It is a great way of sharing and celebrating all the work the children have done together – all their writing can be on display, they can teach pirate skills, show their 'living postcards', sing, dance, eat, drink and celebrate together.

Guidance on assessment

Any assessment of this work will be related back to the Key learning for drama, which stated that by the end of this unit the children will have:

- represented parts of the story using sound, voice and movement – *there are various points at which the children are asked to do this. Do they make images that are consistent with the story? How well do they collaborate in their group to come up with shared ideas?*
- played a game together, following the rules and making suggestions for how the game can be developed – *did everyone join in? Who offered suggestions for commands and actions? How well did they adapt to the game being played in a smaller and smaller space?*
- responded appropriately to the teacher in role, keeping in their own roles as they do so – *did they bring their still picture to life appropriately? When you were being Ted having to learn all his pirate skills, did they respond to you as if you were Ted or as if you were their teacher? How thoughtful and patient were they with their 'pirate teaching'?*
- used locations, costumes and props imaginatively and inventively – *if you use a digital camera for making the postcards, you will have very useful recorded evidence of how well each group met this objective.*

- collaborated to devise a shared party/celebration using music, song, movement and dance as appropriate – *how practical were the ideas? How well could they adapt them for those who came to join them at the party?*

Linking to writing

There are plenty of writing opportunities that arise from this work, including:

- letters, emails and postcards – in particular exchanges between Jed and Farmer Ted where they tell each other how they are doing, and Jed and his pirate family;
- instructions – particularly related to the 'pirate school' and all that the pirates have to learn there;
- log books – notes on where the pirates went, and when, and what they did there.

Adapting this unit

A New Home for a Pirate is one of a number of picture story books about pirates. The unit could easily be adapted for other examples which include:

- *Lila Pirate*, Georgie Birkett, Simon and Schuster, ISBN 978-1-416-91105-0.
- *The Night Pirates*, Peter Harris and Deborah Allwright, Egmont, ISBN 978-1-4052-1161-1.
- *The Green Ship*, Quentin Blake, Red Fox, ISBN 978-0-099-25332-7.
- *The Man Whose Mother Was A Pirate*, Margaret Mahy, Picture Puffin, ISBN 0-140-50624-1.

Many of the structures in this unit – active reading of the text, playing a game related to the story, and sending letters, postcard and emails to and from characters – can be used with lots of picture story books appropriate for this age group.

1C | *The Steel Teddy Bear*

This unit builds on children's science work on materials and their properties.

Where this unit fits in

The Steel Teddy Bear is just one of a number of stories that might be generated by a 'story wheel' activity which mixes materials and the objects for which they are used in playful and imaginative ways. This unit outlines an approach for one possible story, but when you do it with your class, you will find that plenty of others emerge.

This unit connects firmly to the science programme of study at KS1, in particular the expectations that children will be taught to:

- use their senses to explore and recognise the similarities and differences between materials;
- recognise and name common types of material and recognise that some of them are found naturally;
- find out about the uses of a variety of materials and how these are chosen for specific uses on the basis of their simple properties;
- find out how the shapes of objects made from some materials can be changed by some processes, including squashing, bending, twisting and stretching.

Key learning

Key learning for drama

By the end of this unit, the children will have:

- used mime to explore and represent some properties of materials;
- responded in role to teacher questioning;
- worked in pairs and/or groups to create short sections of a story using voice and movement;
- connected ideas from different parts of the drama to make a complete story.

Primary Framework for literacy objectives

- Speaking – experiment with and build new stores of words to communicate in different contexts.
- Drama – act out their own and well-known stories, using voices for characters.
- Creating and shaping texts – independently choose what to write about, plan and follow it through; use key features of narrative in their own writing.

Resources

- Two large sheets of card and a paper fastener to make the story wheel.
- Some metal instruments and other metal objects to make the soundscape.

Although many of the teaching ideas in this unit can be used effectively in the classroom, you will also find it helpful to have access to the hall.

Steps for teaching and learning

Step 1: Exploring materials

This will build on all the work you have done in science exploring a variety of materials through all the children's senses. It is absolutely vital that they have had this first-hand experience before they move on to imagining and representing some of these properties through mime. Get the children to work in pairs, then call out objects and ask them to mime passing them to one another and using them. You can start the game off with some examples of your own – things like a jelly wheelbarrow, a pair of wooden trousers or a rubber ladder – and then ask them to invent ideas of their own. Next try showing a few examples from the pairs and seeing if the rest of the class can guess what they are – the wrong guesses will be just as valuable as the right ones!

Step 2: The story wheel

You need two circles of card, one larger than the other, connected in the centre with a paper fastener. Divide both circles into eight sections. In each of the sections on the inner wheel write some of the materials that the children have been exploring and working with. On the outer wheel add children's ideas for things that would be made using that material.

By rotating the wheel, you will deliberately mismatch the materials and the objects to generate lots of new possibilities. You can continue with the game set out in Step 1, but ask the children to mime one of the options shown on the wheel and then see if the rest of the class can guess what they are showing.

Step 3: Choosing a story to make together

Depending on what the children offer at the story wheel stage, you will be presented with a whole range of possible stories to explore. The story of the rubber table, the wooden hat or the paper ladder

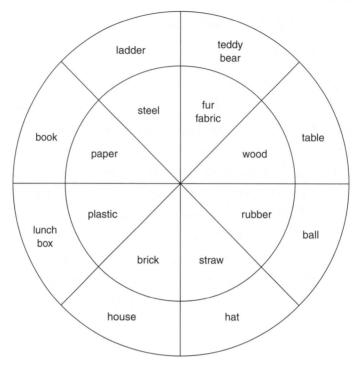

FIGURE 2

would all offer fantastic possibilities. We have chosen the steel teddy bear as an example of how the process of story-making can be developed through drama – the same process could be adapted for a number of other possibilities that the wheel generates. Once children have experienced the process, they may make a number of other 'mixed-up materials' stories they can dramatise and tell, write and illustrate, and then build into a class anthology.

Step 4: Thinking about a steel teddy bear

Talk to the children about the properties of steel that they explored through their science work. What does it feel like? What sorts of sounds can it make? What happens when you scrape two pieces of steel together? Using metal objects, musical instruments and their own voices, children can experiment with making the sounds a steel teddy bear might make. These can be recorded and played back for the movement activity, or you can divide the class in two and have half making the sound while half do the movement, and then swap over.

Accompanied by the 'metal soundscape', the children can experiment moving around the room in the way that a steel teddy bear might. As they are working, get them to notice how their bodies move (slowly, stiffly, creakily?). Catch as much of this language as you can and write it down for future writing. Ask the children how the steel teddy bears seem to feel – do they appear comfortable and happy, or perhaps awkward and ill-at-ease?

Step 5: Meeting the teddy bear(s)

There are a number of options you can take at this stage, depending on how much you feel you need to take control of the overall direction of the story. You may wish to take the role of the teddy yourself and be questioned in role ('hot-seated'), or you may give the role to one or more children to be questioned. A third alternative is for you to meet all of the children in role as a whole collection of steel teddy bears. Whatever option you choose, you will need to introduce the familiar idea from many children's stories that toys can come to life when no one is around. Through questioning the bear(s), they can begin to dig deeper into the story and find out how and why the bears were made, by whom, where they live, etc. Obviously, until you undertake this process with children it is difficult to know exactly what ideas they might come up with, but it is important to stress that working in role is likely to free up ideas in ways that a class discussion will not. If, for example, you decide to take the role of someone who has walked in on the bears by mistake and starts asking them questions about where they live and what they do, you have established that you do not know the answers and therefore any of their responses are valid. The conversations and discussions in role at this stage of the process will give lots of ideas that can be explored and used to build the story later.

Step 6: Building the ideas into a story

You can do this stage of the process either as still images, short mimed/movement pieces or mini-scenes. In small groups or pairs, ask the children to think about how and where the steel teddy was first made. This work can then be shared with the rest of the class and the similarities and differences discussed.

Then ask the children to make an image or scene for the middle part of the story. Where does the steel teddy go next? Does s/he get sent to a shop? What happens if no one wants to buy the teddy? How does the teddy feel during this part of the story?

The third scene or image needs to show how the story ends. At this age, children often expect their stories to have satisfying, happy endings, so encourage them to think about how the teddy might get a new home. Who would want a teddy bear that was different in this way? A child who was allergic to normal fur fabric, perhaps? A tin man who wanted a toy for his tin baby? Once again, until you ask these questions of the children, it is very difficult to predict what sorts of conclusions to the story they might invent, so you need to be open and responsive to all sorts of possibilities.

It is a really good idea to take digital photographs of the children's scenes and/or images and keep them to support later storytelling and writing. Some of them could even be edited using simple software to make the children look more like they are made of steel.

Guidance on assessment

Any assessment of this work will be related back to the Key learning for drama, which stated that by the end of this unit the children will have:

* used mime to explore and represent some properties of materials – *how well are the children able to use their understanding of the properties of materials and the differences between them? Do the mimes reveal new understandings and/or misconceptions?*

- responded in role to teacher questioning – *how you assess this objective, and what sort of understanding the children show, will depend to some extent on the choices you make in Step 5. If you choose to let some or all of the children take roles as the steel teddy bears, how well did they sustain a role? Who invented and improvised imaginative responses to your questions?*
- worked in pairs and/or groups to create short sections of a story using voice and movement – *how well could they work together? How clear were their pictures and/or scenes? Who had particularly good ideas and expressed them clearly and inventively?*
- connected ideas from different parts of the drama to make a complete story – *how clearly can they give you a synopsis of the whole story? How does this translate into their storytelling or writing?*

Linking to writing

As well as writing the story of *The Steel Teddy Bear* or whatever other 'mixed-materials' story you chose to develop as a whole class, children may like to go back to the story wheel from Step 2 and look at some of the other possibilities. Once you have worked through the drama structure with them, they will have a much clearer idea of how they can be playful and inventive with the mix-ups the story wheel generates to create and write more stories of their own.

Adapting this unit

As we have already suggested, this structure can generate a great many more 'mixed-up materials' stories. You could also apply the same sort of overall structure to generating ideas and exploring consequences and outcomes with all sorts of stories. You can, for example, make a story wheel with three rings, and then put the characters, settings and plots from traditional stories on each of them. Mixing these up will generate lots of mixed-up stories to explore, tell and write.

1F | *Jim and the Beanstalk*

This unit is based on *Jim and the Beanstalk*, by Raymond Briggs, Picture Puffin, ISBN 978-0-140-50077-6.

Where this unit fits in

This popular book is a modern sequel to *Jack and the Beanstalk*. Many years have passed since the Giant first encountered Jack and in that time he has aged considerably. His hair and most of his teeth have fallen out and he is finding it incredibly difficult to see. When a beanstalk mysteriously appears in the garden of a boy called Jim, he decides to clamber up and see where it leads. His meeting with the Giant is quite different from Jack's. Although there is an amusing sense of menace (Jim is only safe because the Giant has no teeth), Jim's experiences of modern life improve the Giant's quality of life little by little, step by step. In exchange for the Giant's 'good gold', Jim is able to deliver careful measurements to the optician, the wig maker and the dentist so that the Giant has a set of glasses, a fine new wig and shiny new teeth.

In this unit the story is taken a step further by imagining what might happen if the Giant were to visit. The children create a dinner party for the Giant. They record the event by taking a set of photographs for an album, adding cut-out or computer 'Giant' images once the pictures have been printed.

Key learning

Key learning for drama

By the end of this unit, the children will have:

- used evidence from a text to make decisions;
- explored how it might feel to be a giant living in a tiny world or a tiny person in a giant's world;
- collaborated in groups to create still images for photographs;
- taken photographs of still images;
- used mime to display an imaginary object;
- worked in role to tell the story of the day.

Primary Framework for literacy objectives

- Drama – explore familiar themes and characters through improvisation and role play; act out their own and well-known stories.
- Speaking and listening – retell stories, ordering events.
- Group discussion and interaction – take turns to speak, listen to each other's suggestions and talk about what they are going to do; ask and answer questions, make relevant contributions, offer suggestions and take turns; explain their views to others in a small group, decide how to report the group's views to the class.

Resources

- Digital cameras and access to a PC so that images can be downloaded and printed (preferably one per group of 4/5).
- A number of drapes and cloths for disguising backgrounds.
- A letter from the Giant.
- A selection of images (from magazines, etc.) for children to cut and paste onto their photographs.
- Paper, scissors and glue.

Steps for teaching and learning

Step 1: Getting to know the Giant

Read the story with the children. The next morning, tell them that a letter from the Giant has arrived. Everything about it will need to be extra big; the handwriting, the paper, the envelope – even the stamp. This letter will open up an opportunity to explore something that the book does not: what would happen if the Giant came to visit humans? It might read something like this:

> Dear Villagers,
>
> It is my birthday on Friday and my friend Jim had invited me to a special dinner. I was really excited as it would have been the first time I had attended a birthday dinner in my honour.
>
> Unfortunately, Jim's Great Aunt Beryl has broken her leg and is finding it very difficult to manage on her own so Jim's mum has sent him off to look after her until her leg gets a bit better. As you know, he is very good at looking after people. He tells me he'd much rather have dinner with a giant and I think I believe him.
>
> Jim could tell how disappointed I was, so he suggested that I ask you if you would be prepared to hold a special dinner for me. I would pay for all the food and entertainment. I have good gold.
>
> I look forward to hearing from you.
> The Giant

Discuss whether this is a good idea, encouraging children to draw on evidence from the book. You can write letters back to the Giant where you only agree to the dinner under certain conditions and demand proof that he no longer eats humans.

Step 2: What would it be like for the Giant if he came to visit?

Once your class have agreed to host the dinner, help them to empathise with the Giant by exploring how it might feel to be the Giant living in their land.

Tell the children you are going to play a game called 'Topsy Turvy Land'. This game encourages children to investigate what might happen if someone really big has to deal with a world that, to them, is tiny. It also helps the children to begin thinking about how difficult it would be to play host to a giant.

To play the game, each child finds a space. First you must give them a 'moving through the space' command, but this must be 'topsy turvy'. Some suggestions might be:

* walk in the slowest way you can possibly walk;
* walk without taking your feet off the floor;
* move forward without moving your arms;
* walk without ever moving in a straight line;
* walk around in circles;
* walk around in squares;
* walk without looking at anyone else;
* only walk sideways;
* wobble forwards;
* wiggle backwards.

After a very short time, say 'Topsy Turvy'; this is the prompt to stop and stand still. You then call out some things for them to mime on the spot. These might include:

* drink a whole bottle of pop as quickly as you can using an egg cup for a cup;
* stir a cake mix with a wooden spoon and bowl that are as tall as you;
* fit a wig onto a giant's head;
* put a pair of glasses on a giant's head;
* eat a cake as small as a pea;
* eat a sweet as big as your head.

Step 3: Word from Jim

Introduce an email from Jim, expressing how pleased he is that the class is holding the dinner, but how disappointed he is to be missing out on all the fun. He asks the class if they can take photographs of the event and either email them back or send them in an album.

Step 4: Starting the photo album

Producing a photo album of the Giant's dinner introduces a sense of audience that will make the children far more aware of how important it is to make their images look good. In groups, the children can create images of the dinner and take photos of them, leaving a space where a 'giant' object can be added afterwards. One simple way to do this is to cut pictures from magazines and stick them onto the photos once they have been printed. Alternatively, the children can take a second picture of an everyday object that might be needed at the dinner, photograph and print it, then cut it out and add it to their original. This process is illustrated in Figures 3 to 5:

Figure 3

Figure 4

Figure 5

Depending on the ICT skills and the software you have available, the children can import their pictures into a program such as Textease and combine their images that way.

As a class, discuss the events that would be likely to occur if a giant came to dinner and then decide on some 'photo opportunities'. Encourage each group to find a good background for photographs – disguising equipment with colourful cloths and drapes may be all that is needed. The pictures they create might include the following:

Cooks:

* adding giant spoonfuls of ingredients;
* stirring huge pots;
* working as a team to knead the dough for an enormous loaf for the sandwiches;
* spreading butter on a piece of bread as large as a bed sheet;
* using a giant-sized oven that they have had to build outdoors;
* working as a team to lift and pour from huge pots;
* icing a giant cake.

Waiters:

* setting the table, being aware of the perils of carrying enormous, razor-sharp knives and forks;
* working as a team to spread out a tablecloth the size of a parachute;
* working in pairs to carry very tall candlesticks;
* lighting the candles using a taper as tall as a person;
* folding napkins the size of a bedspread;
* working together to carry out each course for the Giant.

Entertainers:

* juggling with balls the size of beach balls;
* singing through a megaphone;

- climbing up a ladder to tell jokes into the Giant's ear;
- using giant puppets to create a puppet show.

Amusing accidents:

- getting caught under his huge bottom when he sits down;
- being blown over by his sneeze;
- being deafened by his loud voice;
- being shaken about every time he laughs.

Step 5: Producing the photo album

If the children are going to use the computer to paste images onto the top of their photographs, set up a picture file with a selection of useful pictures that they will find easy to access. Programs such as Textease or Easiteach have folders that are easy to open within the program and have large, clear, colourful pictures organised in useful categories such as food, animals, people, etc. For this part of the lesson, children should work in pairs, each having no more than two pictures to annotate. Once they have finished, save their pictures into a shared file where you can open them up in front of the class and turn it into a slide show to send to Jim.

If you decide that the children are going to physically cut and paste images such as plates or cups onto the picture, think carefully about the size that you decide to print them – make sure they are not too small because the children are likely to get frustrated if the photographs are too fiddly to work with. The children will also need a selection of pictures to choose from so they can cut them out and paste them onto the photographs.

When the children have finished cutting and pasting their giant images onto their photographs, you might stick them as they are into an album. The completed pictures can also be scanned (or just photographed with the digital camera) and then be printed on photographic paper or set up as a rolling slide show in a program such as Textease or PowerPoint.

Step 6: A visit from Jim

Finally, the teacher or teaching assistant can take on the role of Jim, who has finished looking after his aunt and has come to find out as much detail as he can about what happened on the day. He is thinking of asking him to dinner again, and the class seemed to do such a good job that he wants further advice. Use the pictures themselves as a talking point – projecting them onto a screen or interactive whiteboard might be the best way to do this. The children will enjoy this last part of the process. Not only will it encourage them to think creatively and imaginatively, but they will feel like experts in a completely new field.

Guidance on assessment

Any assessment of this work will be related back to the Key learning for drama, which stated that by the end of this unit the children will have:

- used evidence from a text to make decisions – *do the children use examples from the story to back up their suggestions?*
- explored how it might feel to be a giant living in a tiny world or a tiny person in a giant's world – *how clearly do the children portray each Topsy Turvy action? How well do they stay in role as they work through each scenario?*
- collaborated in groups to create still images for photographs – *how well do the children respond to the camera? Does this affect the shape of the image that they make?*
- used mime to display an imaginary object – *are the children able to portray the size of the object through their bodies? Can they use expression in their faces to show how awkward the objects are?*
- worked in role to tell the story of the day – *are the children able to recount the story in role to a small audience?*

Adapting this unit

The basic structure of this unit, with its simple but creative use of ICT, could be applied to all sorts of stories where scale and difference in size is important. These might include the elves at work in *The Elves and the Shoemaker*, the original story of *Jack and the Beanstalk* or perhaps the fairies in *A Midsummer Night's Dream*.

1P The King with Dirty Feet

This unit is based on *The King with Dirty Feet: An Indian Tale*, by Pomme Clayton, from *The King With Dirty Feet and Other Stories From Around the World*, edited by Mary Medlicott, Kingfisher, ISBN 978-0-753-45165-6.

Where this unit fits in

Bath time is no everyday activity for the King in this Indian folktale. It is an event attended by all his subjects, who join a long and colourful procession to follow him to the river. This is because for him a bath is extremely rare, making him the very smelliest of sovereigns.

Though there is great celebration once the King has bathed, an unfortunate problem occurs. Despite all the ceremony of the long-awaited soak, he does not remain completely clean for long; the second his feet touch the dusty earth they become dirty again. This infuriates him greatly and he demands a solution from Gabu, the hapless servant who is in constant fear of having his head chopped off.

Gabu makes some interesting suggestions. The first involves sweeping, the second washing and the third – the best of all – creating a beautiful carpet that will stretch to the very edges of the land. But as is so often the way in folk or fairy tales, it is a wise old man watching from afar who finally offers the most obvious and practical suggestion. While the King is standing on the beautifully sewn carpet (which has covered all the plants) the wise man simply takes a pair of scissors, cuts around the King's feet, ties on some string and so creates the first ever pair of shoes – a pair literally fit for a King.

This story can provide a big question in science such as, 'What would happen if we made a carpet to cover the whole of the earth?' which leads to exploration about what living things need to survive. You might also develop children's making skills, using your technology lesson to design the first pair of sandals based on the information they have in the story.

Developing this as a play with young children can work really well when created through improvisation This unit explores how to develop the script through role play then provides a final summary of how the performance might be put together.

Key learning

Key learning for drama

By the end of this unit, the children will have:

- collaborated in pairs and groups to explore ideas for a performance;
- collaborated as a large group to create a soundscape;
- worked with and responded to the teacher in role, making suggestions as appropriate;
- made suggestions for ways in which their work can be turned into a performance for an audience;
- reviewed, reflected on and refined their work for a performance;
- taken part in a performance for an invited audience.

Primary Framework for literacy objectives

- Speaking – retell stories, ordering events using story language.
- Group discussion and interaction – take turns to speak, listen to each other's suggestions and talk about what they are going to do.

- Drama – explore familiar themes and character through improvisation and role play; act out their own and well-known stories using voices for characters; discuss why they like a performance.
- Understand and interpret texts – visualise and comment on events, characters and ideas, making imaginative links to their own experience.

Resources

- A performance space where children can explore ideas and rehearse the play.
- A sound or image of water (optional).
- A crown.
- A cloak.
- Instruments or carefully sealed small drinking bottles containing water.
- Colourful cloths for spreading across the stage.
- A pair of sandals cut out of material.

Steps for teaching and learning, part one: developing a script through improvisation

Step 1: Introducing the story

The room should be set up to show that the children are near an imaginary river – a projected image or the sound of water will be enough to create this. Explain that someone very important is about to come here to this river – a King who is due to arrive for his bath. It is a very special event. Everyone from the village is invited and must join the procession.

You can now take the role of Gabu and tell the next part of the story. Put a cloak around your shoulders to show that when the cloak is on, the children are listening to Gabu, and introduce yourself. Explain that, for those people who have never been in the procession before, this is a very important occasion:

You poor things – you won't be used to it. The King has not had a bath for a long time. He smells terrible, so hold onto your noses! But be warned. If he ever turns around you'd better stop holding your nose! If he sees you insulting him, he will be furious!

Take off Gabu's cloak and take the role of the King by putting on his crown. Ask your subjects if they are ready to follow you on the journey to the Royal bath. Walk the perimeter of the room, moving slowly and majestically with the children following. Tell the children that if you stop and turn round, they must immediately stop holding their nose and bow to you.

Invite children to volunteer to take your place as the King. Then put the cloak back on and become Gabu. Each time the child who is playing the King turns around as they lead the procession, model how to react through Gabu. Encourage the children to think of the phrases the King might say as he turns around, e.g. 'Who has the Royal soap?'

Step 2: The Royal bath

The bath itself does not need to take up a lot of performance time, but it is significant and occurs twice in the story. So it is worth spending time exploring how to present this special event. A really exciting way to play this part of the story is to have the children producing a soundscape of the King washing.

You could use voices or unpitched instruments to produce your watery soundscape. But you can also use unusual instruments – for example, we have used small, tightly sealed drinking water bottles with water inside them.

Model the possibilities – what sound does the bottle/instrument make if you move it gently side to side? If you tap, shake, roll or scrape it? Ask the children to explore the sounds they can make but give them constraints, e.g. make two sounds without tapping, make two sounds

61

without shaking, make a ripple, make a swish. Children will be more open to the variety of sounds that can be made for performance. Gather the children in front of you and ask the children to be very still and silent, and to place the bottles in front of them – the King is soon to arrive.

In role as the King, press your hands together in a praying style. Explain to the children that they are your musicians and you are going to 'call for a sound'. You will announce the sound you want them to make, but while your hands are pressed together there should be absolute silence. As soon as you open your hands to catch the sound, they play it; as soon as your hands come back together, they must stop.

The children's sound must be as long or as short as the King's hand movements. Call out typical sounds that you might hear someone make when they are having a bath:

> Plip
> Plop
> Swish
> Scrub
> Swash
> Plipperty plop
> Plunge
> Drip

Next, explain to the children that the signal they must look for now is the King's action. The sound starts and finishes when the action does. You will describe the action before you make it, then the children will decide at which point to make the sound. For example:

> There will be a gentle 'plip' as I place my first toe in the water.
> A hard 'plop' as I step right in.
> As I sit in the water it will swish around me in a big wave.

Finally, try making the actions without the description. The children will be getting more used to using the actions like a musical score. Eventually, the child you have chosen to play the King can take over the role – once they have seen it modelled, they will be able to pick up the easy step-by-step actions and create their own.

After this, the King will need some grand words to show he has completed the wash, e.g.:

> The King is now CLEAN.

The child who is the King can decide what they would like to say.

Talk to the children about how the villagers would react. They may suggest applause, or a gasp of delight. Encourage them to respond to each other, rather than just looking straight ahead.

This celebration needs to be contrasted with the dreadful moment that the King's feet have become instantly dirty – even after all that washing!

Step 3: Cleaning the earth

In the story, Gabu and the villagers first try sweeping, then washing the land. But the children can create their own solutions. Build the script through role play. Put on Gabu's cloak and ask the children for ideas:

> The King has given me an impossible task. How shall we clean the earth?

Organise children into groups of three or four and ask them to mime different ways of cleaning the ground. Gabu can then walk around the work that is taking place and ask them about their progress. For example, if Gabu approaches a group that is sweeping the land, he might start to cough and comment on how clean the ground is but how cloudy the air is. The child you have chosen to play Gabu should walk around with you to begin with, then they can move off on their own, trying out their own questions. Finally, gather all the children together and list all the ideas that have been suggested.

Explain that you are going to choose two ideas for the story; neither should work, but the second should be more successful than the first. Decide as a class which you will use in the play. Obviously, it is important to keep the third solution the same as in the story – the wise man has to cut into the carpet to make the shoes.

Step 4: The first pair of shoes

Out of role, tell the children the last part of the story – Gabu and the villagers decide to create a leather carpet that will cover the land. Ask the children to find a space in the room and ceremoniously wrap Gabu's cloak around your shoulders. Now, as Gabu, order the children to work as quickly as they can to stitch the cloth together, this is your last chance to please the King. Then join in yourself, talking about how tough it is to pull the needle through the leather and how blistered your fingers have become.

Ask the children to think about how they will react when they finish all the hard work. Discuss what sort of reaction will be most effective for the audience: one big collective sigh, or all the villagers showing individual reactions – try out both.

In the story, the King is delighted to find his feet perfectly clean. This is a dramatic moment, so ask the children how this could be created. For example, the King's final bath could take place in slow motion and in silence. Out of role, explain that the King is going to say what he thinks. The villagers must be ready to react – what will they do if he is furious again? What will they do if he is happy?

Put on the crown and, as in the story, walk across the land and talk about how pleased you are and how splendidly you think Gabu has worked.

Help the children to create the sounds of celebration. Then, out of role, explain that you want the villagers to continue to celebrate, but a new character is going to come into the story. As he passes each villager, they will be silenced one by one because he will have a particular presence and they will not have noticed him before. Ask two children to step into the roles of Gabu and the King.

Become the old man, moving slowly towards the King, winding in and out of the villagers who should gradually quieten their din and look. The children will do this quite readily as they will be keen to know the last part of the story.

Bow before the King and tell him how beautiful the carpet is but ask whether anyone has noticed the unfortunate problem. Allow the children to respond. Talk about how it is impossible for anything to grow because all the living things on the ground are completely covered. Then take out an imaginary pair of scissors and pretend to cut through the carpet around the King's feet to make the first pair of shoes.

Steps for teaching and learning, part two: the play

The following summary provides a suggested outline for the play with possible actions. The lines given in italics are just examples: you and the children will have decided on the actual lines and movements from your earlier work.

Scene 1: The procession

The King walks ahead, occasionally turning around to make demands, e.g. *'Where is the royal soap?'*

Gabu follows the King, turning around to shush the villagers in case the King catches them being disrespectful.

Villagers join the procession, complaining and muttering about the smell. The minute he turns to face them, they appear respectful. They form a circle around the bath.

Scene 2: The Royal bath

The King performs five washing actions.

Gabu stands beside the King and hands him all the things he requires.

Villagers form a circle around the King and, using instruments or sealed bottles, make water sounds to accompany the King's actions.

The scene ends with a grand statement, e.g. 'The King is now clean ...'

Scene 3: Cleaning the earth

The King proclaims, 'The King is clean, but the ground is dirty!'

He turns to Gabu for help: 'You must rid the land of dust or "zut!"'

Gabu turns to the villagers: 'How can we rid the land of dust?'

Villagers suggest their ideas: 'We will wash the land!'

At Gabu's command (possibly with background music), the children playing the villagers will act out the task, quickly and energetically.

For any task that involves using water, they can use their sealed bottles or instruments to make an effective swishing noise. Afterwards, they will show how tired out they are, wiping sweat from their brows and leaning on each other for strength.

Gabu exclaims: 'Get ready for the King!'

Villagers form a circle around the bath and slowly place their bottles in front of them (it will be very effective if they can all do this at exactly the same moment).

The King is furious because the so-called solution has caused a problem bigger than having dirty feet. He roars: 'THERE IS NOWHERE TO TREAD, THE LAND HAS TURNED INTO A SEA!' Then he orders Gabu to try something else.

Gabu and villagers tremble in the face of the King's rage. This chain of events should be repeated again with the second solution, e.g. brushing the land.

The scene ends when the King tells Gabu that he has one last chance. Gabu poses his question once more, and a villager makes a suggestion: 'I know what we'll do! We'll sew a cloth over the whole land.'

The King, Gabu and all the villagers (carrying the bottles with them) leave the stage.

Scene 4: The carpet

Gabu leads the villagers onto the stage.

Villagers carry colourful cloths onto the stage, open them up and spread them out. They walk around on hands and knees pretending to stitch together the pieces of cloth.

The King walks into the space, filled with wonder. He takes one last bath, repeating his five actions. It will be particularly effective if there is a contrast to the liveliness of his first baths, so we suggest it is silent and in slow motion, as this will heighten the suspense.

Gabu and villagers are still, focusing on the King's actions.

The King steps slowly onto the beautiful colourful carpet and inspects his feet. He looks at Gabu, then his subjects, then jumps into the air with a noisy squeal of delight.

Gabu and villagers celebrate noisily.

The Wise Old Man will appear as if from nowhere, walking in from the back of the audience. As he passes the villagers, one by one they will be silenced as they turn to watch. Eventually there will be complete silence as the Wise Old Man finds his way to the King. He will stop, bow, then point out the big mistake: 'Though the ground looks beautiful, nothing will ever grow again because the earth is covered with cloth.'

Have a pair of cloth sandals already made in the same material as one of the sections of cloth the children have laid out on the stage. Make sure the King is standing on this particular cloth – it should be placed right in the centre of the stage.

The Wise Old Man will produce a large pair of pretend scissors and mime cutting the carpet. He will then lift the ready-made sandals, taking them to the King and tying them on his feet.

The King celebrates, trying out different movements with his shoes on. This works well with music.

Villagers and Gabu all follow the King, copying his actions.

The Wise Old Man is left on stage, shaking his head, then exits slowly.

Guidance on assessment

Any assessment of this work will be related back to the Key learning for drama, which stated that by the end of this unit the children will have:

- collaborated in groups to explore ideas for a soundscape – *to what extent are children able to explore a range of sounds and link this directly to action on stage?*
- worked with and responded to the teacher in role, making suggestions as appropriate – *how imaginative are the children in role and how clearly did they express their ideas?*

- made suggestions for ways in which their work can be turned into a performance for an audience – *to what extent could children think about sharing their work with an audience and understand how this might be different from performing for themselves?*
- reviewed, reflected on and refined for a performance – *how well do children respond to direction and are they able to adapt and improve their performance? Can they identify elements that need improvement?*
- taken part in a performance for an invited audience – *how well can children maintain being in role in front of an audience. How much acting do they do on stage?*

Adapting this unit

The basic structure of exploring the themes and ideas of a story through drama, then using these as the basis for performance work, could be used for lots of stories. Clearly it lends itself very well to traditional tales, but you could use it with almost any story you and your class are working on.

2L | *The Lost Happy Endings*

This unit is based on *The Lost Happy Endings*, by Carol Ann Duffy and Jane Ray, Bloomsbury, ISBN 978-0-747-58106-2.

Where this unit fits in

This award-winning, beautifully illustrated book asks an intriguing question: what would happen if all the happy endings from stories were lost? Every day a little girl called Jub goes out into the forest and collects all the happy endings that were used up the previous night when children heard their bedtime stories. These are all gathered together and tied up in a special sack. One night as she carries the stories back through the forest, she is attacked by an old witch who steals them all. There is not a glimmer of a happy ending in any of the stories told at bedtime that evening so it is essential that Jub reclaims the sack as quickly as she can. Eventually she finds the witch and the happy endings, managing to save them the second before the witch casts them into a bonfire. In the end, it is the evil witch who comes to a frazzled end.

This literacy-based unit leads to a piece of written work describing Jub's journey through the forest, ending at the moment when she loses the sack – the children decide how it has been lost. You might also consider making other curricular links. You might want to create an outdoor art display based on the pictures in the book where happy endings hang like streamers from the branches of trees.

Children would also enjoy looking at stories that do not necessarily have happy endings – English legends and folktales rarely do! You might also consider the way that some stories change over time while others remain the same for hundreds or thousands of years, such as the narratives captured in religious writing – which, interestingly, do not always have happy endings.

Key learning

Key learning for drama

By the end of this unit, the children will have:

- worked imaginatively in pairs to decide what might be contained in the mysterious sack;
- worked in groups to form tableaux of different story endings;
- worked in large groups to create a soundscape;
- used adventurous language in a word carpet.

Primary Framework for literacy objectives

- Speaking – explain ideas and processes using imaginative, adventurous vocabulary and non-verbal gestures to support communication.
- Listening and responding – listen to others, ask relevant questions and follow instructions.
- Group discussion and interaction – work effectively in groups by ensuring that each group member takes a turn challenging, supporting and moving on.
- Drama – adopt appropriate roles in small or large groups and consider alternative courses of action; consider how mood and atmosphere are created in live or recorded performance.

> ## Resources
>
> As well as a copy of the book, you will need to put together a sack which contains a selection of last lines from stories. You will also need three different types of atmospheric music: happy, sad and mysterious.
>
> Towards the end of the unit, the class will be split into halves to make a soundscape. In order to do this, you may need the help of an extra adult.

Steps for teaching and learning

Step 1: The mystery sack

Prepare the room before the children enter, so that there is a sense of mystery and expectation as they walk in. In the centre of the space, place the sack under a spotlight (an overhead projector would do the job) and play some soft, interesting music.

Ask them to walk around the room, looking for spaces, keeping a close eye on the sack. As they are walking around the room they should think of one thing – *who has this come from?* While the children move, play three short extracts of music in the background; one sad, one cheerful, one spooky. At the end of each (you should play each extract for no longer than 20 seconds) ask the children to stand very still. Turn the lights off and walk in and out of the children with a torch. When the light of the torch is cast on them, they should call out who they think the sack might belong to. The ideas will change with each piece of music. Reassure the children that if they don't have their own idea when the light of the torch is cast on them, they can call out the last thing they heard, or use a default decided by the class such as 'wise old gentleman'.

Step 2: Playing with objects

The first thing you can get the children to do is to create their own stories about what might be contained in the sack. The atmosphere that has been created in the room will prepare children to be more imaginative in their thinking. As a class, form a circle around the outside of the sack. Explain to the pupils that they are going to play a miming game called 'What is it and what would I do with it?'

If you have another adult working with you, ask them to be your partner so the children can watch how the process works; otherwise, ask a child to volunteer. The first person mimes opening the sack and takes something out; for example, a top hat. They tell their partner what it is, acting out and saying what they are going to do with it, e.g 'I am going to use the hat as a Frisbee' – their partner must receive it in an appropriate way. The second person then mimes opening the sack and repeats the process. The opening of the sack is important, because it gives the children thinking time to help them decide what might be in the sack.

Step 3: The sack of happy endings

The children will be so excited by their own ideas that they will have almost forgotten that there is actually something inside the sack. This is the time to open it up and reveal that it contains a selection of happy endings. At this point, do not read the happy endings to the children, as you will be giving them out shortly. Instead, read the first part of the story, explaining how Jub collects them every day so that she can send them back out into the night ready for when the stories are read at bedtime.

Organise the children into groups of four or five. Give a 'happy ending' to each group and ask them to form a still image of it. Use story endings from traditional tales such as *Goldilocks and the Three Bears* or *Cinderella*. When the children have had time to explore and create their tableaux, direct the class to look at each in turn, showing them how to 'read' what they see. You might ask questions such as:

- How is this character feeling? How can you tell this from looking at them? What can you see in their body language?

- What do you think has just happened?
- What might happen next?

Exploring physical expression helps children to use adventurous language in their writing. Using a phrase such as 'He gripped the ring tightly in his fist' can be more effective than saying or writing 'He didn't want to lose the ring.'

Step 4: The missing page

Explain to the children that there is a page missing from the book, which describes the moment when Jub wanders into the mysterious forest carrying the sack, and then, somehow, loses it. Say to the children that you cannot remember exactly how the sack was lost.

The children are going to be writing the missing part of the story, opening it with her journey into the mysterious forest where she is startled and unnerved by all the sounds and shadows around her, ending it by explaining how she lost the sack. Tell the children that, to help them, you are all going to create the forest setting together.

Step 5: Forest soundscape

Now you are going to make a soundscape to help children to think of language to describe the forest. Discuss how Jub might feel as she walks through the dark woods. Does the dark make her notice things that she would not have noticed before?

Divide the class into two groups; an adult will need to work with each group. Explain that they are going to create a picture of the forest for the other group, using their voices. Discuss which sounds Jub may have heard in the forest; everything from gentle, eerie noises that would make her ears prick up, to startling sounds that would make her jump. Talk about how a really good atmosphere can be created by using silence as well as sound; a sudden stillness can introduce suspense and uncertainty. Explain why too much repetition of the same sound (such as whistling, screaming or howling) can really spoil the atmosphere, since it becomes a predictable irritation rather than something unexpected.

When you have had a good discussion about sound quality, ask the children to get into pairs. Each pair needs to create a sound that Jub hears in the forest. They must do their best to try to think of a different sound from those they are hearing others make.

Once all the sounds have been created, listen to each one and then start making some decisions about how these will be performed. The first thing to consider is where you will want the other half of the class to be placed when the soundscape is performed for them. Should they be scattered around the room with their eyes closed? Should they be led through the soundscape? Should they be sitting in a circle with their eyes closed and the lights turned off? This decision will affect how and where the sounds are performed.

Next, reflect on the sounds the children have created, and decide as a group which ones you will want to make together as a whole group (such as gentle pitter-pattering on the floor), which will need to move (like the sound of the wind moving in and around the 'audience'), and which will need to be done individually (perhaps the sudden sound of footsteps running through and around them).

Give the children the opportunity to practise the soundscape several times. The teacher and teaching assistant may decide to act as a conductor to keep the action going, or they may be able to choose a confident child to do the same job. Whatever you decide, there will need to be someone who will keep the children focused on the order of sounds and movements that need to be made.

When the soundscapes are performed, ensure that the 'audience' is very still and silent before it begins. Soundscapes work particularly well if the audience listens with their eyes shut because they begin to picture and imagine what might really be in the forest. Emphasise that if they feel uneasy at any time, it is perfectly acceptable for them to open their eyes.

Step 6: The word carpet

After the children have experienced the soundscape, have a quick discussion about the things they might have heard in the magical forest. You can also talk about the effect that the soundscape had on their bodies. For example, they might say things like, 'I hugged myself tightly' which is a very good way of portraying the fear that Jub might have had as she moved through the forest.

Give out some pieces of paper (about A5 size) and thick marker pens or crayons. The children write down one phrase per piece of paper and it must be big enough for others to read. They are going to create the forest using a carpet of words, spread across the floor of the hall where they are working. Make it clear that although they should not focus too much on spelling, they should be adventurous with their language. You might expect phrases such as 'Singing wind' or 'Chattering insects', but not simply 'Trees' or 'Shaking'. Encourage the more able to consider using phrases that describe their fear through their body language.

When the word carpet has been produced, ask the children to move back into pairs. Tell them that they are going to choose four ideas from the word carpet to create a description of Jub's journey through the forest. They must then use three phrases that will connect these ideas. Choose the phrases most appropriate for the children to work with – you may choose to differentiate them for different groups. They might choose phrases like: 'As soon as …'; 'Every now and then …'; 'Suddenly …'

Through speaking and listening to each other and using the ideas from the word carpet, the children will be starting to construct a story that uses sequencing and the type of time language used in familiar stories. They will be practising connectives that they can use in their own writing and also developing their ability to use more adventurous language. You can then use this rich beginning as an inspiration for children's extended writing.

Guidance on assessment

Any assessment of this work will be related back to the Key learning for drama, which stated that by the end of this unit the children will have:

- worked imaginatively in pairs to decide what might be contained in the mysterious sack – *how varied are the children's ideas? How well do they respond to each other when working in pairs?*
- worked in groups to form tableaux of different story endings – *how well do they communicate with each other in groups? Does every child have a role?*
- worked in large groups to create a soundscape – *who contributes? How well can they control the sounds they use?*
- used adventurous language in a word carpet – *how much of the language they have used through drama have they been able to transfer to their written work?*

Adapting this unit

The soundscape and word carpet structure in this unit could be adapted and applied to lots of books and stories across the 4–7 age range.

2C Light and dark

Building on from children's science work on light and dark, this unit also draws on work on life processes and living things, thinking about nocturnal and diurnal animals.

Where this unit fits in

Children at this age are expected to understand 'that darkness is the absence of light' and this can be a difficult idea for some. This unit plays with the idea of days getting shorter and shorter until there is only night-time left, and the animals in the story are left in perpetual darkness. Through their roles as the animals in the story, the children devise a solution to the problem.

This unit connects firmly to the science programme of study at KS1, in particular the expectations that children will be taught:

- to identify different light sources, including the Sun;
- that darkness is the absence of light.

Many schools will make 'Light and Dark' a cross-curricular theme or topic to include literature such as *Owl Babies* or *The Owl Who Was Afraid of the Dark*, and work on nocturnal and diurnal animals.

Key learning

Key learning for drama

By the end of this unit, the children will have:

* used sound and movement to explore and represent a wood at night;
* responded appropriately to the teacher in role;
* collaborated to create and enact a meeting of the animals;
* worked from their roles to explore the central problem of the story and suggest possible solutions and outcomes.

Primary Framework for literacy objectives

* Listening – listen to others in class, ask relevant questions and follow instructions.
* Group discussion and interaction – listen to each other's views and preferences, agree the next steps to take and identify contributions by each group member.
* Drama – adopt appropriate roles in small or large groups and consider alternative courses of action; consider how mood and atmosphere are created in live or recorded performance.

Resources

* A good space, preferably the hall, which can be darkened to create an appropriate atmosphere for the story.
* Something to represent an old tree stump – the log base from an old Christmas tree will do very well, or you may simply cover a small PE bench with a piece of cloth.
* A 'story stick' to use as you narrate the story with the children – an old walking stick will do, but it is great if the stick looks old and worn as if it has told many stories.
* A puppet of a day-time animal, for example a squirrel (optional).

Steps for teaching and learning

Step 1: Thinking about animals of the day and night

Begin by talking to the children about what wild animals they know about, which ones prefer day and which night. Explain that the story you are going to make together happens in a wood. Ask the children to find a space and then think of an animal they would like to be. Tell them that when you tap your 'story stick' on the ground three times the wood is going to come alive and the animals are going to move through it, but if you hold the stick and call 'story stick', they must stop in the middle of what they are doing and hold their shape perfectly still. Play this game two or three times, commenting on the animals you can see represented and the things you can see them doing.

Next you can experiment with using light to signal day and night. You need do nothing more than turn the lights on and off. Start by asking the children to be animals that are active in the day and sleep at night. When the lights are on they move around the wood; when the lights are turned off they curl up and pretend to sleep. Then tell them that you want them to be animals that come out at night and play the game again, this time waking when the lights are off and sleeping when they are on.

Step 2: Introducing the story

Use the story stick to narrate:

> There was once a wild and beautiful wood which was full of animals. Some of the animals liked to come out in the day, and some at night. Living like this they all got along very happily and lived well in their wood for many years.

> Then one autumn something very strange began to happen. The days grew shorter and the nights longer, just as the animals

expected. But this year the shortening of the days just went on and on, until at last there seemed to be no day at all, only night. Dark, dark night.

Step 3: Meeting the squirrel

At this point in the story you may want to introduce the squirrel puppet as a character. Seating the children close to you, give them the opportunity to question the squirrel. Explain that the squirrel is very nervous and shy, and that she seems to be very worried about something. Ask the children to begin speculating why – if they were following the story earlier they are likely to speculate that she is anxious about the disappearance of the daylight but, if not, you can bring this out through your responses to their questioning.

There are a number of ways the puppet can respond to the children's questions. You may decide that she will only nod or shake her head to answer: carefully framing their questions for such a response can be a lovely challenge to set children. But you can also have the puppet 'whisper' the response in your ear or perhaps in the ear of the child who asked the question. Whatever you decide, you need to get across that the squirrel is very worried and does not know where to turn for help.

If you do not want to use the squirrel puppet, you can take the role of Squirrel yourself and respond directly to the children's questions. A really simple piece of costume such as a pair of knitted gloves can help to signal to the children that you are in role as Squirrel.

Step 4: The meeting of the animals

Another piece of narration moves the story on to the next stage:

> In the middle of the wood there was an old tree stump. This was a very special place for the animals for they believed it to be all that remained of the first tree ever to grow in their wood. If ever

they needed to meet and talk, the animals would gather around the tree stump.

Seat the children in a circle and place the tree stump in the middle. Explain that when the animals meet, only the one who is on the tree stump is allowed to speak. If an animal wants to talk to the others, s/he must go and stand on the stump, speaking loudly and clearly so everyone can hear. When s/he has finished, any other animal that wishes to speak must signal by holding up a paw. The animal that has just spoken will then get off the tree stump, go and touch the paw of the next animal to speak, then take their place in the circle. This gives the meeting a strong sense of ritual and importance. The room will now need to be darkened for the meeting to take place.

Step 5: Squirrel comes to the meeting

As Squirrel, you now take your place on the tree stump. From there you tell the other animals how you have noticed the days getting shorter and shorter, how difficult you find it to cope with the darkness, and how you are quickly running out of food. There is obviously something very wrong and you need the help of all the animals to know what to do next.

When you have finished speaking, step down off the tree stump and choose the next animal to speak – you will almost certainly find that several have raised paws! It is essential that you and they respect the rules of the meeting, and that no one speaks unless on the tree stump.

As the meeting develops, the children will come up with lots of ideas about what has happened and what the animals should do about it. We have done this piece of work in a number of schools and there are several directions the story may take. They may begin by suggesting ways in which the night animals can help the day animals while the darkness lasts. One class suggested building a large fire to light part of the wood up; another moved more into the realm of myth and sent birds to fly up and find the source of the problem.

Until you start the meeting, it is very difficult to predict what your class may come up with.

Step 6: Enacting the end of the story

Having listened carefully to the children's ideas, you can narrate their ending of the story while they act it out as the animals. Use the story stick again, sometimes calling 'Story stick!' to freeze the action and talk about what is happening.

Guidance on assessment

Any assessment of this work will be related back to the Key learning for drama, which states that by the end of this unit the children will have:

- used sound and movement to explore and represent a wood at night – *at the beginning of the drama who contributes well to this activity and who finds it difficult?*
- responded appropriately to the teacher in role – *this will be particularly important in Steps 3 and 5 when you take the role of Squirrel. How readily do they accept you being in role? Do they stay in their roles as the animals when they respond to your input at the meeting?*
- collaborated to create and enact a meeting of the animals – *did they follow the rules? Who contributed?*
- worked from their roles to explore the central problem of the story and suggest possible solutions and outcomes – *what suggestions were made from the tree stump? How well did they build on each other's ideas?*

Linking to writing

When you have finished this drama, you can go through the main stages and talk to the children about how the whole story of *The Dark, Dark Night* fits together. This will provide an excellent structure for their own writing.

2F The First Snow of Winter

This unit is based on *The First Snow of Winter* from Silver Fox Films.

Where this unit fits in

The First Snow of Winter is a delightful animated tale from Ireland. Frequently shown on network television around Christmas, it features the voices of Miriam Margolyes and the late Dermot Morgan. The film tells of a duck called Sean who becomes separated from his family as they fly south for the winter. He has an accident which means he cannot fly and must somehow survive the cold winter. He is befriended by Vole who helps him to prepare for the winter ahead. But when Vole goes off to hibernate, Sean must face the dangers alone. It is a story of friendship and survival that will appeal to children of this age, offering them plenty of opportunities to reflect on how this story is told through film and the devices the film-makers use to engage and elicit responses from the audience. The film is widely available on DVD.

This unit might connect to other work you are doing on traditional stories – although this isn't a traditional tale as such, it has many of the features of one and there is much to explore about characters, setting and plot. Obviously, the winter setting of this film echoes the moods and feelings of that time of year: it would work very well as a short unit around Christmas, or perhaps at the start of the spring term.

Key learning

Key learning for drama

By the end of this unit, the children will have:

- created a series of tableaux in response to the film, speculating on how the plot might develop;
- developed a sequence of movement in response to a section of soundtrack from the film;
- improvised and refined dialogue based on stills from the film;
- explored some of the differences between film drama and their own live work.

Primary Framework for literacy objectives

- Speaking – tell real and imagined stories using the conventions of familiar story language; explain ideas and processes using imaginative and adventurous vocabulary and non-verbal gestures to support communication.
- Listening and responding – respond to presentations by describing characters, repeating some highlights and commenting constructively.
- Drama – present part of traditional stories, their own stories or work drawn from different parts of the curriculum for members of their own class; consider how mood and atmosphere are created in live or recorded performance.
- Understand and interpret texts – give some reasons why things happen or characters change.

Resources

- A copy of the film, preferably on DVD because the pause/still function is so much better, and a way of projecting it clearly – an interactive whiteboard would be ideal.
- Digital cameras are very useful for recording the children's work which can then be shown on screen and compared with the original film.

Steps for teaching and learning

Step 1: Exploring the opening

Begin by playing the title music without the pictures. The children can immediately begin to speculate what sort of film they think it might be and what sort of story it might tell. Even if some of them have seen the film before, they are unlikely to recognise it from the music alone. Do not spend long talking about the music before you introduce it with the film. Pause the film as the title appears over an image of birds flying in an autumn sky, then talk about what the children are now beginning to think about the film. At this point you may get some children who tell you they have seen the film before: tell them you are really pleased to hear it and that their knowledge will be really useful as the work develops, but that they should try not to tell everyone what happens.

Step 2: Sean and Puffy

Sean the duck and his friend Puffy the puffin are the first two characters that appear. Their relationship becomes clear very quickly with Sean the adventurous risk-taker and Puffy the more cautious voice. After looking at the first few minutes of the film, up to the point where Sean escapes the fox for the first time, put the children into pairs and ask them to think of other scrapes and adventures Sean and Puffy might have got into. Initially these can be presented as still images, but the work can be extended by asking the children to add words and movement to create a very short scene. It can be a very good idea to set a maximum number of words the scene may contain (around ten would be best) so that the work is tight and focused. You can also impose the discipline of the work starting and finishing with a still (still–move–still). Putting these short scenes together may take some time, but they will really encourage the children to think about the two characters and extend what they already know from the film. At this point, it can also be a really good idea to give children still and/or video cameras to record their work, encouraging them to think about where the camera will see the action from and giving you the opportunity to introduce some film language such as long-shot, close-up, zooming and panning.

Step 3: Sean and his family

The first few minutes of the film also reveal a great deal about Sean's family: his anxious mother, his laid-back father and his two beautifully-behaved siblings. There is a really good opportunity here to hot-seat some of the characters to explore their feelings and attitudes more deeply. Depending on the experience of your class, you may like to take one of the roles yourself first to model how the process works. If you take the role of mum, for example, and invite the children to ask you about Sean, his dad and his sisters, try to include references to some of the incidents they invented in Step 1. This will not only help validate and celebrate their work, it is also a very good lesson in how drama can help us to look more deeply into the story behind the story seen on the screen.

Step 4: The accident

Form a circle and ask one of the children to step into the middle and take the role of Sean. Provided you can see the screen from where you form the circle, pause the film just before Sean's accident, where he is all alone in an empty sky. Tell the children you are going to use your voices to create the sounds and feelings of that moment. If you begin with sounds, they will need to be mostly soft and whispery – take some time and trouble to get this right. The sounds can then inform the words you use to describe how Sean is feeling and, just as importantly, the ways you say them: 'lost and alone', for example, or 'silent and scared' can be spoken in the circle in long, slow whispers. In the same way that the film soundtrack does, the children can then experiment with building these voices into the sound of the on-coming aircraft which sends Sean tumbling from the sky. At this point they will need to build their voices into the loud roar of the aircraft, before speaking words like 'tumbling', 'falling', 'dipping' and 'dropping' as Sean falls towards the ground. As the class use their voices to create the sound and mood of Sean's accident, the child in the middle responds through movement. Once your sound piece is finished, you can try adding the film soundtrack over it.

Step 5: Meeting Vole

As with the others in the film, the character of Vole is established very quickly. He begins by trying out a couple of his ideas to get Sean airborne again and flying south for the winter. Both of these ideas include him saying, 'Did I ever tell you about the time I was … ?' Rather as they did in Step 1, children can think of other ways in which Vole might have tried to help, and represent them as short scenes/images. Not only will this encourage inventive and imaginative ideas from the children, it will also get them thinking about Vole and the kind of character he is. You can use a similar structure to explore some of the ways in which the friendship between Sean and Vole develops. In the film Vole is shown teaching Sean how to make a sound with a blade of grass, and the two of them are shown dancing together. Children will readily think of other things they learn and do together – you may even have a child who learns Irish dancing and can teach you some of the steps.

Step 6: Escaping from the fox

About 15 minutes into the film, there is a scene where Sean and Vole are pursued by a fox. Play the soundtrack of this section of the film, but without the picture showing, and ask the children to think about what might be happening. In groups of three or four, get them to represent their ideas as three still images. Then get them to build movement between the images so that it fits with the film soundtrack. You will need to play the soundtrack repeatedly while they practise and refine their work, but the sequence only lasts for just over a minute so you will be able to repeat it several times for them. In this sequence Sean and Vole will need to hide. This is a really good opportunity to talk to the children about how they represent their 'hiding' in drama. Rather than actually going to hide behind or in things, encourage them to show how they are hiding through body shape and posture. Similarly, the 'chase' part of the sequence does not need to involve everyone tearing around the hall at speed – show them how their movement can be planned and carefully controlled.

Step 7: Vole breaks some news

Some 16 minutes into the film, Vole has to tell Sean that they will not be together all through the winter because voles have to hibernate. Pause the film just as Vole is about to tell Sean something – it is very clear from his expression and 'body language' that he has something difficult to say. Put the children into pairs and ask them to represent the image on screen; one as Sean and the other as Vole. When you give the command 'Play', the pairs improvise the conversation between the two until you say 'Pause'. Keep the improvisation short, but be prepared to run it more than once. Hear some examples from the children, then play the film and compare the similarities and differences.

Step 8: The winter storm

This is another great opportunity to create a soundscape, rather like you did in Step 4. If you can get hold of a large Wellington boot like the one in the film, one of the children can represent Sean making his way towards it while the others use their voices to make a mixture of verbal and non-verbal sounds that drive Sean back and away from it.

Step 9: Meeting Puffy

Play the section of the film where Sean finds his friend Puffy in the snow. It shows not only how Sean saves Puffy, but also how he teaches him all that he learned about friendship. In pairs, the children can create either still images or short scenes between Sean and Puffy. These will be rather like those they made with Sean and Vole, only this time you can ask them to finish their scene with a statement about friendship: 'A good friend will always ...' or 'A good friend should ...'

Step 10: The battle with Fox and the family re-united

Watch the last part of the film to the point where Sean is re-united with his family. In groups, get the children to improvise this meeting, then get the child who plays Sean to tell the story of what happened to him over the winter. How do his family react? What stories do they have to tell of their own winter in the South? What has each of them learned?

Linking to writing

Clearly, there are lots of opportunities for writing, both as the project progresses and after you have finished. Writing as Sean, children could keep a diary at various stages. The children can also be introduced to simple script-writing, using some of their improvised dialogue as a starting point. Any of the sections of film that you have explored together can be used to stimulate narrative writing.

Guidance on assessment

Any assessment of this work will be related back to the Key learning for drama, which stated that by the end of this unit the children will have:

* created a series of tableaux in response to the film speculating on how the plot might develop – *how effectively do they make these? How far do they reflect their understanding of the film and its plot?*

* developed a sequence of movement in response to a section of soundtrack from the film – *how well do they plan and control these? Can they adapt and match their movement to the soundtrack?*

* improvised and refined dialogue based on a still from the film – *does their dialogue fit with the film? Does what they say move the story on? How well does what they say reflect the characters in the film?*

* explored some of the differences between film drama and their own live work – *what observations do they make about these differences? Are they beginning to see that film-makers, like writers, make choices and that the children's ideas can be just as good?*

You are very unlikely to want to record detailed answers to these questions for all the children, but you may want to record something about those that performed very well during the work, and/or those who found it difficult to engage.

Adapting this unit

This unit is just one example of how film can generate and stimulate active drama work. Many of the structures and strategies outlined here could be applied to almost any film that is suitable for this age range.

2P | *A Midsummer Night's Dream*

This unit is based on *A Midsummer Night's Dream*, by William Shakespeare.

Where this unit fits in

This is one of Shakespeare's best-loved and most frequently performed plays. It is particularly the world of the fairies and the tricks they play on humans that will appeal to children of this age, and creating and exploring this world can be a delightful way to introduce them to Shakespeare's stories and language.

The plot is complex and can be challenging to explain clearly and simply. This unit sees the play's plot through the eyes of the fairies and through Puck, who is servant to Oberon, King of the Fairies.

How much of Shakespeare's language you choose to use as you develop this unit, and how much you expect the children to learn for their eventual performance, is up to you. But it is very important to stress that children at this age are encountering new words and new language all the time and they are likely to cope with some of the original text much more readily than we might think. It is also worth remembering that the patterns, rhythms and rhymes of the language help children to commit it to memory.

A larger-scale project on *A Midsummer Night's Dream* might include:

- researching forests and woods and the plants and animals that live in them – although the play describes 'a wood near Athens', it is clear from the text that Shakespeare has based much of the play on the Warwickshire woodlands, plants and animals that he knew.
- researching the jobs (carpenter, joiner, weaver, bellows-mender, tinker, tailor) that the mechanicals do and what their lives might have been like in Shakespeare's time.
- designing and making the set for the play – the work in the unit is mainly set in the wood and there is plenty of potential for looking at examples of how woods have been shown in other productions of the play. The Royal Shakespeare Company's website (www.rsc.org.uk) has plenty of pictures of past productions to help children's thinking.

Key learning

Key learning for drama

By the end of this unit, the children will have:

- collaborated in pairs and groups to explore ways of creating a forest through sound and movement;
- worked with and responded to teacher in role, making suggestions as appropriate;
- made suggestions for ways in which their work can be turned into a performance for an audience;
- reviewed, reflected on and refined for a performance;
- taken part in a performance for an invited audience.

Primary Framework for literacy objectives

- Speaking – speak with clarity and use appropriate intonation when reading and reciting texts.
- Group discussion and interaction – ensure that everyone contributes, allocate tasks, and consider alternatives and reach agreement.

- Drama – adopt appropriate roles in small or large groups and consider alternative courses of action; consider how mood and atmosphere are created in live or recorded performance.
- Understand and interpret texts – give some reasons why things happen or characters change.

Resources

Decisions about where you might want to stage your production will probably need to be taken quite early. Many schools now have outdoor performance areas and, if the time of year is right, this could be ideal for this story. If you are going to perform in a hall, think about where and how it might be best to seat the audience. You will want to make sure they are as close to the action as possible, and the structures suggested in the unit may lend themselves to seating the audience on four sides of the performance.

Although you can rehearse in all sorts of spaces, including your classroom when necessary, children will benefit from spending time with you in the actual space where they will perform so that they can make their own suggestions for how the play will be staged.

This version should need only one set which will be the wood near Athens. This can be as simple or complex as you want it to be. If you are short of ideas, just take a look at some images of past productions on the Internet and you will see that there are countless ways of representing a wood. The same goes for costumes, but do encourage children to think about the kinds of mischievous fairies they are and decide on costumes accordingly – the traditional 'fairy outfit' may not do the job!

Steps for teaching and learning

Step 1: Creating a forest through sound and movement

Start from the fairies' song in Act II Scene 2:

> You spotted snakes with double tongue,
> Thorny hedgehogs be not seen;
> Newts, and blind-worms, do no wrong;
> Come not near our fairy queen
> Weaving spiders, come not here;
> Hence, you long-legg'd spinners, hence!
> Beetles black approach not near;
> Worm nor snail, do no offence.

Divide the children up into six groups and give each a creature (or two) from the song (spotted snakes, thorny hedgehogs, newts and blind worms, weaving spiders, beetles black, worms and snails). Ask groups to devise a repeated movement for their creature(s) and practise combining speaking the names of the creatures with the movement they have devised as they move through the space. Review each group's sound and movement, and then experiment with combining them and asking the whole class to move and freeze on a given signal from you.

Next you can introduce an instrument to accompany each group. The children listen carefully and only move if their instrument is playing – if it is not, they must hold the still they were in when it stopped. To make this work most effectively, you may need to take a musician from each group and experiment with different ways of combining the instruments and movement. By the end of this activity you will have a piece of sound and movement that evokes the atmosphere of the forest. You can experiment with lighting it in different ways. If you are in the hall, this may involve little more than closing the curtains, trying different lights on and off, adding some spotlights if you have them, even shining a powerful torch across the moving image of the forest. And you can point out to the children that they have already all spoken some of Shakespeare's words, and have what could be a very effective opening to their performance.

Step 2: What fools these mortals be!

Discuss with the class what sort of forest they have created. Would it be an exciting place to go? Would it be scary? Why? What might it be like to be lost in the forest at night? Explain to the children that the fairies who live in the forest are mischievous and enjoy playing tricks on the humans who come into their world. What sorts of tricks do they think the fairies might play?

Divide the children into groups again and ask each to think of a trick that the fairies might have played on someone. Ask them to show their trick in a short mimed scene, emphasising that the humans should not be able to see the fairies. Then ask them to add a line telling everyone what they have done, for example:

>   We tripped the mortals up and made them fall

or perhaps

>   We stole the mortals' food and ate the lot

As each group comes up with their line, work with the class to see if they can all be made to fit the same rhythmic pattern – this will be very useful for the next stage.

Step 3: The meeting of the fairies

Seat the children in a circle and tell them that this is going to be the special place where the fairies meet to celebrate all the tricks they have played and all the fun they have had. Introduce Puck's line from Act II Scene 1:

>   How now spirit! whither wander you?

Get the children to repeat the line with you several times, listening for the rhythm in the language. Then stand in the circle and experiment with different ways of clapping and stamping this rhythm, sometimes with the words, sometimes without. Once you have established a way of performing the line over and over as a whole class, you can add in the groups' work from the last activity. As the circle performs 'How now spirit! whither wander you?', the first group comes into the middle of the circle ready to perform what they did to the mortals in their wood. Once they are in place, the rest of the circle fall silent and still, and listen and watch the group's movement and line. When the group in the middle have finished, the rest of the class repeat their line (e.g. 'We tripped the mortals up and made them fall'), then clap, laugh and cheer at all the fun they have had. Then the circle resumes the 'How now spirit! whither wander you?' chanting and clapping while the group that have just performed leaves the circle and the next one comes in.

When all the groups have been into the middle and performed, you and the class will have created a delightful and powerful introduction to the world of the fairies which can be built into your eventual performance. Although you will have given an overall structure, the piece will be built primarily from children's own work and ideas.

Step 4 (optional): Introducing Puck through teacher in role

This step offers children the opportunity to gather something of the plot while staying in their role as fairies. You tell the story by taking the role of Puck and joining the other fairies in their circle to tell them all about the tricks you have played.

Get them to perform their 'How now spirit!' piece again, and then come into the middle of the circle and say you have great things to tell them about, but you will need their help to show what happened. As you tell the story, bring children into the circle to take the roles of the characters you describe.

Tell them how Titania, their Queen, and Oberon, their King, have fallen out. He wanted to play a trick on her, so he sent you to get a special flower. The juice of this flower can make someone fall in love with the first thing they see. Oberon puts the juice on Titania's eyes while she was asleep. Then you saw some workmen rehearsing a play in the wood. There was this one man who seemed to want to do everything and be everyone in the play, so you thought you would play a trick on him. You took him away and gave him the head of a donkey! Then you left him where Titania would find him when she woke up. Now she has fallen in love with this great ugly beast and Oberon is very pleased with you!

Come out of role and talk to the children about the story. Do they think it was a good trick to play? What do they think might happen next? You can also begin to talk to them about how they want to show this bit of the story in their eventual production. Then tell them that Puck comes to the fairies' circle for a second time, only this time he is not so happy.

The second time you come to the circle as Puck you can tell the story of the lovers, Helena and Demetrius, and Hermia and Lysander. Tell how Oberon saw Helena chasing Demetrius through the wood. She loved Demetrius, but he did not love her. Oberon felt sorry for Helena and told you to put some of the flower juice on Demetrius' eyelid so he fell in love with her when he woke up. He told you that you would know which one was Demetrius 'By the Athenian garments he hath on'. The trouble is there was another Athenian man in the wood that night. His name was Lysander and he also had Athenian garments on, so you put the juice on his eye by mistake. He was already in love with Hermia (and she with him), but when Lysander woke up the first person he saw was Helena so now he is in love with her instead! Then you tried to put it right by putting some juice on Demetrius' eye and he woke up and also fell in love with Helena. So now they are both in love with Helena, and no one is in love with Hermia. Helena and Hermia are supposed to be friends but now they are just fighting and arguing with each other. Oberon is very angry and you don't know what to do. Have the fairies got any ideas?

As the children (in their roles as fairies) come up with ideas for what Puck could do, they come into the middle of the circle and, just as you did when you told your stories, bring other children into the circle to act out roles so that they can explain what they think needs doing.

Using the strategy of teacher in role here allows you to turn the complexity of the plot to your advantage. Through your role as Puck, you can show yourself to be very confused about it all, and give the children the role of sorting it out with you. It also allows you to tell the story of the lovers, but to keep it light-hearted and fun in a way which is entirely appropriate for this age group. It is a very engaging and enjoyable way of introducing the plot that will help with all the later work on the play.

Step 5: The fairies tell the story

Now they know the basic elements of the plot, you can begin to talk with the children about how they would like to tell the story in the performance. Do they want to keep the idea of the fairy circle and tell the story in that? Perhaps they want to break out of the circle and perform the story in another way. Either way, it will be very helpful to involve the children in all of these decisions, so that they feel they own the performance with you rather than just doing as you tell them.

As they tell the story, there will probably be some key scenes you and they will want to include and through which you can introduce some lines from the play:

Oberon tells Puck to get the flower:

OBERON: Fetch me that flower; the herb I showed thee once:
The juice of it on sleeping eyelids laid
Will make man or woman madly dote
Upon the next live creature that it sees

PUCK: I'll put a girdle round about the earth
In forty minutes

The mechanicals rehearse their play:

QUINCE: Is all our company here?
FLUTE: Nay, faith, let me not play a woman; I
have a beard coming
SNUG: Roar!
BOTTOM: Let me play the lion too
(After Puck has put the donkey's head on Bottom)
ALL: O Bottom, thou art changed!

The lovers come into the wood:

DEMETRIUS: I love thee not, therefore pursue me not!
HELENA: I'll follow thee and make a heaven of hell

Puck mixes the lovers up:

LYSANDER: Not Hermia, but Helena I love
HELENA: Wherefore was I to this keen mockery born?
HERMIA: O me! you juggler! you canker-blossom! you thief of
love!

Titania wakes up and falls in love with Bottom:

TITANIA: What angel wakes me from my flowery bed?

Puck sorts the lovers out

PUCK: Jack shall have Jill;
Nought shall go ill;

If you know the play, you recognise that some of these suggested lines
and events are not in the exact order they appear in the play. They
serve only to suggest a structure for the fairies telling their story. You
will need to work with your class to see how you and they want to
bring them to life. You may want to leave some of the lines out,

perhaps add or substitute others. What matters most is that the eventual performance grows out of the drama work we outline, and draws on all the children's suggestions and ideas as they go.

Step 6: The fairies make amends

To draw their telling of the story together, the fairies' circle can create a group performance of the lines that Puck speaks at the end of the play:

> If we shadows have offended,
> Think but this, and all is mended,
> That you have but slumber'd here
> While these visions did appear.
> All this weak and idle theme,
> No more yielding but a dream,
> Gentles, do not reprehend:
> If you pardon, we will mend.

You can give one line to each group and ask them to devise a way of performing it together. Then, rather like the fairies telling each other about their tricks at the start, they can create a dynamic, shared performance of the lines with which to end.

Guidance on assessment

Any assessment of this work will be related back to the Key learning for drama, which stated that by the end of this unit the children will have:

* collaborated in pairs and groups to explore ways of creating a forest through sound and movement – *this objective relates to the work right at the beginning of the unit. You will have plenty of opportunities to observe how imaginative children are with this task and how disciplined they were as they performed it. Could they listen for and follow signals? How effectively did they manage the transitions from movement to stillness?*

- worked with and responded to teacher in role, making suggestions as appropriate – *if you choose to work in role as Puck, you will get plenty of insight into how the children respond in role; who comes up with appropriate and imaginative responses?*
- made suggestions for ways in which their work can be turned into a performance for an audience – *this is a key element of this unit. To what extent could children think about sharing their work with an audience and understand how this might be different from performing for themselves?*
- reviewed, reflected on and refined for a performance – *as you get nearer to a performance, you will find you are becoming more and more demanding of the children in this area. But there is nothing wrong with that – you and they should want their work to be the best that it could possibly be.*
- taken part in a performance for an invited audience – *we often talk of children 'rising to the occasion'. This is an important skill – how well did they hold the performance together for their audience?*

Adapting this unit

Although *A Midsummer Night's Dream* is often considered the most suitable of Shakespeare's plays for children of this age, the structures we have outlined could be adapted for others; for example, *The Tempest* or perhaps *Romeo and Juliet*. The storytelling structures that are used throughout can be used for turning all sorts of stories into performance.

Appendix 1

Drama structures and strategies used throughout the book

Freeze/move

Children 'free-play' some action from the story and 'freeze' when told to by the teacher. This creates instant images of the story. It can be a really good idea to capture these with a digital camera, either as evidence of what you did or perhaps to illustrate later writing.

Improvising dialogue

Usually done in pairs, the children take roles and improvise the conversation that happens between them. This can often lead to writing, perhaps putting the dialogue into a story, or writing it for a playscript. See, for example, Unit 2F, *The First Snow of Winter*.

Inventing games

This can be a very effective and playful way of engaging children with the themes and ideas of a story. The 'pirates' game, for example, which is played in Unit 1L, *A New Home for a Pirate* can be easily adapted for another context as in Unit RL, Castles.

Letters and messages

These can be introduced as a way of moving the story on, adding surprise, excitement or tension. See, for example, the note from the princess in Unit RL, Castles or the email from Jim in Unit 1F, *Jim and the Beanstalk*.

Meeting in role

The children sustain their roles while they meet together and discuss what has happened in the story/drama and what they should do about it. See, for example, Unit 2C, Light and dark, when the animals meet.

Soundscapes

Using their voices, sounds they can make with their bodies, everyday objects and/or musical instruments, children create mood and atmosphere with sound. See, for example, Unit 2L, *The Lost Happy Endings*, or Unit 1C, *The Steel Teddy Bear*.

Still images or tableaux

A very widely used strategy in which children make pictures using themselves. These might show people (or perhaps animals) doing something, or they may be more abstract, as in the wood the children create in Unit 2P, A *Midsummer Night's Dream*.

Teacher in role

Used in many of the units, the teacher takes a specific role within the drama and engages in 'live' action with the children. It is a very powerful strategy from which you can question, challenge and extend children's thinking and understanding.

Word carpets

Words and phrases developed through the drama are written on scraps of paper and put out on the floor to create a 'carpet' of words. These might be used to create a setting, or developed further into mood and atmosphere as in Unit 2L, *The Lost Happy Endings*. They are very useful resources for later writing.

Writing in role

Children write as if they were characters in the story. For example, they might write letters home from Ted the farmer in Unit 1L, *A New Home for a Pirate*, or reply to Jim's email in Unit 1F, *Jim and the Beanstalk*.

Appendix 2

Further reading to help develop drama in your school

Ackroyd, J. and Boulton, J. *Drama Lessons for Five to Eleven-year-olds*. David Fulton 2001. Highly practical, detailed and well-structured lesson plans, some for this age group.

Dickinson, R. and Neelands, J. *Improve Your Primary School Through Drama*. David Fulton 2006. A detailed and uplifting account of how one inner-city primary school placed drama at the heart of its curriculum with remarkable results. Plenty of practical advice and examples.

Winston, J. *Drama and English at the Heart of the Primary Curriculum*. David Fulton 2004. Detailed plans with thorough underpinning theory. Examples are included for all the primary age groups.

Winston, J. and Tandy, M. *Beginning Drama 4–11*. David Fulton, 3rd edition 2008. A very practical guide, aimed at those who are new to teaching drama and designed to lead you through the process step-by-step.

Index